The Catholic Biblical Quarterly
Monograph Series
31

45

The Structure of 1 Maccabees

BY

David S. Williams

The Catholic Biblical Quarterly
Monograph Series
31

For Rachel

Produced in the United States of America

ISBN 0-915170-30-2

Contents

Acknowledgments

There are several persons whom I wish to thank. Dr. George Howard read an early draft and made a number of excellent observations. I also appreciate all the good comments, suggestions, and corrections made by the editor of the series, Dr. Michael Barré, and the reviewers who read the manuscript. Any errors that remain are, of course, my own.

My dear wife, Jen, was unflagging in her support at every point of my research and writing. The final stages of the book's production were accompanied by the arrival of our daughter, Rachel, and the thrill of watching her progress through each new phase of her young life. It is with pleasure that I lovingly dedicate the book to her. Finally, I must thank the world's greatest dog, Schnecken, for keeping my feet warm as I sat at my desk.

David S. Williams
Department of Religion
University of Georgia
Athens, GA 30602

CHAPTER 1

Introductory Concerns

The Purpose of this Study

1 Maccabees opens with a brief account of the career of Alexander the Great (1:1–9). The book then presents a forty-year period of events, stretching from the accession of Antiochus IV in 175 BCE to the death of the Jewish leader Simon in 134. In 1:16–64 various measures taken by Antiochus against the Jews and their religion are recounted, including the desecration of the Jerusalem temple; the construction of a citadel, near the temple, which was garrisoned by Greek soldiers; and the suppression of the Jewish cult.[1] A description of a rebellion against these measures, spearheaded by Mattathias, a priest, then follows in 2:1–70. Three of Mattathias' five sons figure prominently in the remainder of the book, and they usher in the Hasmonean dynasty, from the family name.[2] From 3:1 to 9:22 Judas (Maccabeus) leads the Jewish revolt. He is followed, after his death, by Jonathan, whose deeds

[1] On the desolating sacrilege set up by the Greeks in the temple, which is mentioned in 1 Macc 1:54, see D. Wenham, "Abomination of Desolation," *ABD* 1. 28–31. The location of the citadel (the Akra) has been a thorny problem. For representative discussions, see K. Kenyon, *Jerusalem* (New York: McGraw-Hill, 1967) 113–14, 135, 142; and A. Legendre, "Jérusalem," *Dictionnaire de la Bible* 3/2 (1912) 1368–70.

[2] On this family, see T. Rajak, "Hasmonean Dynasty," *ABD* 3. 67–76. J. Sievers (*The Hasmoneans and Their Supporters. From Mattathias to the Death of John Hyrcanus I* [South Florida Studies in the History of Judaism 6; Atlanta: Scholars, 1990] 28–29) examines four explanations of the family's name and concludes that a decision about its origin is impossible on the basis of the available evidence.

are depicted largely in 9:23–12:53. Finally, the leadership of the last of the three, Simon, is described in 13:1–16:24. The book closes with Simon's son, John Hyrcanus, becoming his successor.[3]

Based on the syntax of 1 Maccabees, as well as some evidence of mistranslations, it is commonly accepted that the book was originally written in Hebrew.[4] It exists now, however, only in a Greek translation, together with versions in Latin, Syriac, and other languages. The book is typically dated to ca. 100 BCE. The upper limit appears to be provided by the death of John Hyrcanus in 104, since the final two verses of the book seem to summarize his accomplishments. The lower limit is set by the very favorable depiction of the Romans in 1 Maccabees 8, which presumably would not have been written following the conquest of Judea by Pompey in 63.

1 Maccabees has received a great deal of attention, but scholarly interest has focused on issues involving various historical matters, and the only literary concerns that have received much treatment have been the book's poetry and its unity.[5] Recently, N. Martola has attempted to offer a corrective to this

[3] Major studies of the historical period covered in 1 Maccabees may be found in the following works: B. Bar-Kochva, *Judas Maccabaeus: The Jewish Struggle against the Seleucids* (Cambridge: Cambridge University, 1988); E. Bickerman, *The God of the Maccabees: Studies on the Meaning and Origin of the Maccabean Revolt* (SJLA 32; Leiden: Brill, 1979); K. Bringmann, *Hellenistische Reform und Religionsverfolgung in Judäa: Eine Untersuchung zur jüdisch-hellenistische Geschichte (175–163 v. Chr)* (Göttingen: Vandenhoeck & Ruprecht, 1983); T. Fischer, *Seleukiden und Makkabäer* (Bochum: Brockmeyer, 1980); L. L. Grabbe, *Judaism from Cyrus to Hadrian* (2 vols.; Minneapolis: Fortress, 1992); D. Harrington, *The Maccabean Revolt: Anatomy of a Biblical Revolution* (Wilmington: Glazier, 1988); E. Schürer, *The History of the Jewish People in the Age of Jesus Christ (175 BC–AD 135)* (4 vols.; rev. and ed. G. Vermes, F. Millar et al.; Edinburgh: Clark, 1973–87); Sievers, *The Hasmoneans*; and V. Tcherikover, *Hellenistic Civilization and the Jews* (Philadelphia: Jewish Publication Society, 1961). For a convenient survey of scholarly thought on the causes of the Maccabean revolt, including the works of Bickerman, Tcherikover, J. A. Goldstein (*I Maccabees* [AB 41; Garden City, NY: Doubleday, 1976]), and Bringmann, see Grabbe, *Judaism from Cyrus to Hadrian*, 1. 247–256.

[4] See P. Joüon, "Quelques hébraïsmes de syntaxe dans le premier livre des Maccabées," *Bib* 3 (1922) 204–6. Among the commentators, the following are particularly interested in pointing out Semitisms in the Greek text: C. Grimm, *Das erste Buch der Maccabäer* (Leipzig: S. Hirzel, 1853); W. Oesterley, "The First Book of Maccabees," *APOT* 1. 67–123; and F.-M. Abel, *Les Livres des Maccabées* (Paris: Gabalda, 1949).

[5] See especially G. Neuhaus, *Studien zu den poetischen Stücken im 1. Makkabäerbuch* (Würzburg: Echter, 1974), and H. W. Ettelson, "The Integrity of I Maccabees," *Transactions of the Connecticut Academy of Arts and Sciences* 27 (1925) 249–384. An important issue which

lack of attention to literary issues, by delivering a study of the composition of the book.[6] In the present work I will seek to expand this new interest in studying 1 Maccabees from a literary point of view, and will address the issue of the book's literary structure, by which I mean the network of relations among its parts.[7] As will be seen, Martola and I address similar issues and obtain some similar results, but we use different methods.[8] I will spell out the similarities and differences between Martola's work and my own as I proceed.

Scholarly Views of the Structure of 1 Maccabees

It will be helpful to begin this study by reviewing previous scholarly opinions concerning the disposition of 1 Maccabees. Since Martola has given us the first special treatment of the division of the book, and because his study is so important to my own, I will concentrate on his work in what follows.

There is virtual unanimity among scholars in regard to the division of 1 Maccabees. The standard approach holds that the book has four main parts, with the first serving as an introduction to the other three, which are segmented according to the careers of the three prominent Hasmonean brothers. An outline of this typical division follows.

---

combines literary and historical concerns is the chronology of 1 Maccabees. Several theories have been offered to account for the various chronological data in the book. For an overview, see Grabbe, *Judaism from Cyrus to Hadrian*, 265–266. Essentially, there are three major positions. Bickerman (*God*, 101–11) held that there are two systems of dating in 1 Maccabees, one Jewish (which begins the Seleucid era with Nisan 311 BCE) and one Seleucid (which begins with Tishri 312 BCE). K.-D. Schunck (*Die Quellen des I. und II. Makkabäerbuches* [Halle: Niemeyer, 1954]) used Bickerman's notion of two dating systems to perform a source analysis, but he disagreed with Bickerman concerning the Jewish system, which Schunck held begins with Nisan 312. Bringmann (*Hellenistische Reform*, 15–40) asserts that there is only one system of dating in the book, which he argues begins with Tishri 312. These theories produce different understandings of the dating of the attack on Jewish religion under Antiochus IV. Bickerman's position leads to a dating of 167–164, while the positions of Schunck and Bringmann support a dating of 168–165. Judging from recent reference works, Bickerman's theory, which has been the most popular, remains widely accepted.

[6] N. Martola, *Capture and Liberation: A Study in the Composition of the First Book of Maccabees* (Abo: Abo Akademi, 1984).

[7] Cf. S. Bar-Efrat, "Some Observations on the Analysis of Structure in Biblical Narrative," *VT* 30 (1980) 155.

[8] I will explain below that my study employs rhetorical criticism. Martola, however, essentially performs a form-critical investigation.

A. Introduction	1–2
B. Judas	3:1–9:22
C. Jonathan	9:23–12:53
D. Simon	13–16

Martola observes that scholars rarely offer any justification for this structural pattern, and thus he argues that there is a need for a thorough investigation of the division of 1 Maccabees based on literary considerations. He begins his analysis of the composition of 1 Maccabees by breaking the book into its smallest segments, which he refers to as elements. Having isolated the elements of 1 Maccabees, Martola then attempts to synthesize the data, by searching for continuities and connections among the elements. By this means, he links larger and larger sections of what he calls the main story of 1 Maccabees.

In Martola's view the events of 1:16–64 (the series of calamities brought upon the Jews by Antiochus IV) are of signal importance, since they lead to a situation of imbalances. These imbalances point to the *raison d'être* of 1 Maccabees, as an account of events by which the various imbalances were eventually corrected. For Martola, the most important places in the text where corrections occur are 4:36–59, which describes the liberation of the temple, its purification, and the restoration of the cult; and 13:49–52, which is concerned with the liberation of the citadel and its purification. He therefore asserts:

> Seen from the horizon of the first chapter, [1 Maccabees is] above all, the story of the liberation of Jerusalem, in the first hand the liberation of the temple temporarily occupied by foreign powers, secondly the liberation and sanctification of [the citadel] built and inhabited by foreign heathens.[9]

In this light, Martola views the essential components of 1 Maccabees—those pertaining to the main story—to be chapters 1–7; 9–11; and 12:24–14:15. He further holds that 8:1–32, 12:1–23, and 14:16–16:24 are additions to the main story, appearing either as what he calls "islands," having little or nothing to do with their surroundings (8:1–32; 12:1–23), or as material which he claims follows the natural end of the course of events (14:16–16:24). Indeed, Martola asserts that 14:4–15, a eulogy of Simon, who

[9] Martola, *Capture and Liberation*, 201.

led the Jews to victory over the inhabitants of the citadel, provided the ending of the original version of 1 Maccabees.

If the poem at 14:4–15 was originally the end of the book, why, then, does 1 Maccabees appear as it now does? Martola does not attempt to answer this question directly, but he does note how the supposed additions to the main story seem to result in a shift of emphasis. While the hypothetical original edition concerns the capture and liberation of Jerusalem, the expanded version (the present 1 Maccabees) conveys an account of the first generation of the Hasmoneans in general, making the point that the leadership was handed down to a person of the generation following Judas, Jonathan, and Simon. Because of the change of emphasis from the first edition to the expansion, the original ending has been covered over, and the eulogy of Simon has therefore lost its power as a structural boundary. Instead, the parallel between 9:22 and 16:23–24 comes to the fore. 9:22 reads:

> Now the rest of the acts of Judas, and his wars and the brave deeds that he did, and his greatness, have not been recorded, but they were very many.[10]

This sentence seems balanced at the end of the book by 16:23–24:

> The rest of the acts of John [Hyrcanus] and his wars and the brave deeds that he did, and the building of the walls that he completed, and his achievements, are written in the annals of his high priesthood, from the time that he became high priest after his father.

In outlining 1 Maccabees as it now stands, Martola relies on the parallelism between 9:22 and 16:23–24, and divides 1 Maccabees 3–16 into two parts rather than the three (one each for the three brothers) of the standard scholarly division. The two parts deal with: (1) the achievements of Judas (3:1–9:22) and (2) the achievements of Jonathan and Simon (9:23–16:24).

A Critique of Previous Scholarship on the Structure of 1 Maccabees

I turn now to point out what I consider to be a flaw in previous scholarship on the structure of 1 Maccabees, including Martola's work, however helpful

[10] All English translations of 1 Maccabees in the present study are taken from, or are based on, the *NRSV*. All emphases in these translations are my own.

it is on several counts. It is simply this: sufficient notice has not been taken of the role of repetition in the book.[11] The significance of this inattention is that, as "a basic phenomenon in biblical speech, repetition . . . provides the backbone for discerning structures and meanings."[12]

To be sure, scholars have seen some degree of repetition at work in 1 Maccabees. For example, the phrase διεπορεύετο τὰς ἐπάνω χώρας appears twice in the book.[13]

> Then [Antiochus IV] took the remaining half of his forces and left Antioch his capital in the one hundred and forty-seventh year. He crossed the Euphrates river and went through the upper provinces (διεπορεύετο τὰς ἐπάνω χώρας). (3:37)
>
> King Antiochus [IV] was going through the upper provinces (διεπορεύετο τὰς ἐπάνω χώρας) when he heard that Elymais in Persia was a city famed for its wealth in silver and gold. (6:1)

This is a rather simple case, in which repeated wording seems to play a connective role: after 3:37 we do not meet up with Antiochus IV again until 6:1, and the text is reminding us where he is. Some commentators do point out this instance of repetition.[14] Yet, in the bulk of this study I will draw attention to numerous examples of repetition in 1 Maccabees that appear to have struc-

[11] A. Lefèvre ("Maccabées [Livres I et II des.]," *DBSup,* 598) does make the following intriguing observation: "Notre auteur compose selon le procédé cher aux écrivains bibliques, le parallélisme." His further comments, however, are largely limited to 1 Maccabees 1–2.

[12] P. Trible, *Rhetorical Criticism: Context, Method, and the Book of Jonah* (Minneapolis: Fortress, 1994) 102. Cf. A. Berlin, *Poetics and Interpretation of Biblical Narrative* (Sheffield: Almond, 1983) 136. Two major studies of the role of repetition in biblical writings are R. Alter, *The Art of Biblical Narrative* (New York: Basic Books, 1981) 88–113, and M. Sternberg, *The Poetics of Biblical Narrative* (Bloomington: Indiana University, 1985) 365–440. Perhaps the best example of repetition structuring a biblical narrative, given the present topic, is Judith, since, as is the case with 1 Maccabees, it was composed in Hebrew but now exists in Greek. See T. Craven (*Artistry and Faith in the Book of Judith* [SBLDS 70; Chico, CA: Scholars, 1983]), who argues that repetition is the major organizational feature in Judith.

[13] For the Greek text of 1 Maccabees, I have used *Maccabaeorum Liber I* (ed. W. Kappler; Vetus Testamentum Graecum 9/1; Göttingen: Vandenhoeck & Ruprecht, 1936), though in a few instances I have not maintained Kappler's use of capitalization and punctuation. Grimm (*Das erste Buch der Maccabäer*, 59) explains τὰς ἐπάνω χώρας as "die hochgelegenen Länder jenseits des Euphrat"–i.e., Mesopotamia and Iran as viewed from the standpoint of the Mediterranean coastline.

[14] See, e.g., Grimm, *Das erste Buch der Maccabäer*, 91, and Abel, *Les Livres des Maccabées*, 108.

tural importance, but which have gone largely or completely unnoted by scholars.

Let us consider the following case. In 1:5 and 6:8 the same phrase occurs: "he fell on the bed (ἔπεσεν ἐπὶ τὴν κοίτην)." The phrase is noteworthy in that it appears nowhere else in the LXX.[15] In both verses it refers to a king who is about to die: in 1:5, Alexander the Great, and in 6:8, Antiochus IV. The lack of attention paid by scholars to this repetition, however, may be illustrated by the fact that translators of 1 Maccabees tend to use different wording in the two verses to render the repeated phrase. The translations provided by F.-M. Abel are representative: for 1:5 he translates our phrase as "il dut s'aliter," but for 6:8 he has "il se jeta sur sa couche."[16]

This lack of attention to the parallel between 1:5 and 6:8 is striking, given the fact that in addition to the repetition of the phrase ἔπεσεν ἐπὶ τὴν κοίτην there are further correspondences between the settings of the two verses. In the case of Alexander, we read that as he "fell on the bed" in 1:5 he "knew that he would die (καὶ ἔγνω ὅτι ἀποθνῄσκει)," and in 1:6 he "summoned his retainers (καὶ ἐκάλεσε τοὺς παῖδας αὐτοῦ)." Similarly, Antiochus "fell on the bed" in 6:8, in 6:9 "he thought he would die (καὶ ἐλογίσατο ὅτι ἀποθνῄσκει)," and in 6:10 he "summoned all his Friends[17] (καὶ ἐκάλεσε πάντας τοὺς φίλους αὐτοῦ)." Yet only four of the major com-

[15] But cf. Jdt 8:3 (καὶ ἔπεσεν ἐπὶ τὴν κλίνην αὐτοῦ). For statistical data concerning the LXX, I have used the software program *Accordance* (© 1996 OakTree Software Specialists).

[16] Abel, *Les Livres des Maccabées*, 3, 111. (The same translations are found in F.-M. Abel and J. Starcky, *Les Livres des Maccabées* [Paris: Cerf, 1961] 84, 130.) Abel is by no means alone. Indeed, not a single one of the following translations provides the same wording for the phrase ἔπεσεν ἐπὶ τὴν κοίτην in both 1:5 and 6:8: E. Kautzsch, "Das erste Buch der Makkabäer," *Die Apokryphen und Pseudepigraphen des Alten Testaments* (1900; reprinted, Hildesheim: Georg Olms, 1962) 1. 34, 50; Oesterley, "The First Book of Maccabees," 67, 87; H. Bévenot, *Die Beiden Makkabäerbücher* (Bonn: Peter Hanstein, 1931) 47, 88; P. D. Schötz, *Erstes und Zweites Buch der Makkabäer* (Würzburg: Echter, 1948) 5, 25; S. Tedesche and S. Zeitlin, *The First Book of Maccabees* (New York: Harper & Brothers, 1950) 69, 125; J. T. Nelis, *1 Makkabeeën* (Roermond: Romen & Zonen, 1972) 45, 131; J. R. Bartlett, *The First and Second Books of the Maccabees* (Cambridge: Cambridge University, 1973) 19, 80; Goldstein, *I Maccabees*, 189, 306; K.-D. Schunck, *1. Makkabäerbuch* (JSHRZ 1/4; Gütersloh: Gerd Mohn, 1980) 298–299, 323; and W. Dommershausen, *1 Makkabäer 2 Makkabäer* (Würzburg: Echter, 1985) 14, 47.

[17] The term "Friends" is capitalized because it represents an official title and status. In the ancient world the Friends of a king were given privileges associated with members of the royal court. See H. Donner, "Der Freund des Königs," *ZAW* 73 (1961) 269–77, and A. Van Selms, "The Origin of the Title 'The King's Friend,'" *JNES* 16 (1957) 118–23.

mentaries on 1 Maccabees mention at 1:5 and/or 6:8 that there is a repetition of the phrase ἔπεσεν ἐπὶ τὴν κοίτην in the other verse, and in all but one case they simply record this fact with no acknowledgement of the additional correspondences.[18]

1:1–10 and 6:1–17 are recognized by many scholars as literary units within 1 Maccabees.[19] As we have seen, in these two units we may observe similarities of wording and theme as Alexander the Great and Antiochus IV die. When we take further notice of the fact that Alexander the Great is only mentioned in 1 Maccabees at 1:1, 7 and 6:2, and that Antiochus IV is introduced in 1:10 and dies in 6:16, we have an intriguing situation. It seems possible, if not likely, that the two units are linked in some fashion through the use of repetition. It appears, however, that few scholars have seen such a connection. This situation suggests that by not paying due attention to significant repetitions in 1 Maccabees we may be missing important structural clues in the book. This is why I will be concentrating, in this study, on the role of repetition as a structuring device in 1 Maccabees.[20]

[18] The four commentaries are Grimm, *Das erste Buch der Maccabäer*, 6, 93; C. Keil, *Commentar über die Bücher der Makkabäer* (Leipzig: Dörffling und Francke, 1875) 30, 112; Nelis, *1 Makkabeeën*, 45; and R. Doran, *The First Book of Maccabees: Introduction, Commentary, and Reflections* (New Interpreter's Bible 4; Nashville: Abingdon, 1996) 31. It is Doran who recognizes that the phrases "to fall sick" and "to perceive/recognize that he was dying" recur. (He does not mention, however, the summoning of retainers/Friends.) In addition to these four scholars, I consulted Kautzsch, "Das erste Buch der Makkabäer"; Oesterley, "The First Book of Maccabees"; Bévenot, *Die Beiden Makkabäerbücher*; Abel, *Les Livres des Maccabées*; Tedesche and Zeitlin, *The First Book of Maccabees*; J. C. Dancy, *A Commentary on I Maccabees* (Oxford: Basil Blackwell, 1954); Abel and Starcky, *Les Livres des Maccabées*; Bartlett, *First and Second Books of the Maccabees*; Goldstein, *I Maccabees*; Schunck, *1. Makkabäerbuch*; J. J. Collins, *Daniel, First Maccabees, Second Maccabees* (Wilmington: Michael Glazier, 1981); and Dommershausen, *1 Makkabäer*.

[19] See chapter two below.

[20] I am borrowing here from the title of an article by K. I. Parker, "Repetition as a Structuring Device in 1 Kings 1–11," *JSOT* 42 (1988) 19–27. This article engendered a stimulating discussion in *JSOT* 51 (1991). See A. Frisch, "Structure and Its Significance: The Narrative of Solomon's Reign (1 Kings 1–12.24)," 3–14; Parker, "The Limits to Solomon's Reign: A Response to Amos Frisch," 15–21; and Frisch, "The Narrative of Solomon's Reign: A Rejoinder," 22–24. See also J. Walsh, "Symmetry and the Sin of Solomon," *Shofar* 12 (1993) 11–27. In a forthcoming article ("Once Again: The Structure of the Narrative of Solomon's Reign," *JSOT*), I argue that the evidence favors Parker's view of the structure of 1 Kgs 3:1–11:13, though I also show how the structural plans presented by Parker, Frisch, and Walsh support one another and together serve to reveal the rich artistry of the narrative of Solomon's reign.

Methodological Considerations

I will base my study on the methodological suggestions made recently by M. Butterworth.[21] In a review of Butterworth's work, R. F. Person has written that "Butterworth's contribution is his insightful critique of the subjective claims of previous works on the structure of biblical texts."[22] I agree with this assessment and would add that Butterworth has also provided some helpful and sensible guidelines for constructing a more objective approach for structural studies.

Butterworth begins by analyzing some studies of structure in biblical books. His summary comments on one such work, by J. de Waard,[23] are representative of Butterworth's general conclusions.

> [De Waard] has employed unconscious, imprecise criteria in deciding which correspondences are significant with respect to structure; he has apparently ignored some correspondences completely. . . . He does not consider *all* the data available, but is selective and apparently arbitrary. . . . He does not consider alternative theories that might rival his own. He offers no rationale for his procedure, nor criteria for estimating the significance of the available data.[24]

In short, Butterworth asserts that those who have performed structural studies have often operated without objective criteria and proper controls.

Butterworth is not alone in this assessment. Other scholars as well have commented on the lack of methodological rigor in some studies of structure in biblical literature. Of special note, in this regard, are studies that claim to have uncovered chiastic structures, where there are inverted correspondences between words, phrases, or other, more extensive material.[25] For

[21] M. Butterworth, *Structure and the Book of Zechariah* (JSOTSup 130; Sheffield: Sheffield Academic, 1992).

[22] R. F. Person Jr., review of Butterworth, *JBL* 113 (1994) 135.

[23] J. de Waard, "The Chiastic Structure of Amos 5.1–17," *VT* 25 (1977) 170–77.

[24] Butterworth, *Structure*, 39 (author's own emphasis).

[25] On the use of chiastic structuring, see *Chiasmus in Antiquity: Structures, Analyses, Exegesis* (ed. J. W. Welch; Hildesheim: Gerstenberg, 1981). In his introduction to this volume, Welch claims that the following are important objective criteria of a chiasm: repetition; balance; inversion; a focus or shift at the center; and the density of the parallel forms. S. Bar-Efrat (*Narrative Art in the Bible* [JSOTSup 17; Sheffield: Almond, 1989] 98 n. 2) has suggested that we distinguish "between a ring or envelope structure (A .... A), a concentric structure (A,B,x,B,A) and a chiastic structure (A,B,B,A)." While I believe that this suggestion has merit, I have not seen it

instance, R. B. Dillard remarks: "Occasionally after reading an article suggesting a chiastic structure for a given passage, one is left with the feeling that it was all done with mirrors, that the labels had been sufficiently doctored as to yield the desired results."[26]

M. J. Boda has recently taken the step of assembling a list of frequent errors made by analysts who claim to have identified chiastic structures in Hebrew compositions.[27]

1. Sometimes, there is a lopsided design for a chiasm. The length of matching units can vary widely.
2. Some postulated chiasms are irregular in arrangement, and must therefore be treated with caution.
3. Techniques and structures which have been discovered in more than one passage of a work are more reliable than those which appear only in the particular passage at hand.
4. Some variables in a chiasm seem to have been arbitrarily deemed significant, while other items that do not fit a scholar's pattern are rejected.
5. Individual section limits seem set to fit a pattern and are not manifest in the text.
6. Items are arbitrarily labelled.
7. Alternative explanations for a structure are bypassed, such as when patterns are simply part of the natural arc of a narrative.
8. Too much emphasis is placed on high frequency words and/or technical terms especially related to the subject matter of a passage.
9. Some linguistic features, such as gender and number of nouns, and conjugation and mood of verbs, may form patterns by accident.

---

widely adopted in the scholarly literature. Therefore, to avoid confusion, in this study I will use the terms chiasm and chiastic structure to refer both to what Bar-Efrat would call a concentric structure and to what he would call a chiastic structure.

[26] R. B. Dillard, "The Literary Structure of the Chronicler's Solomon Narrative," *JSOT* 30 (1984) 86. Cf. J. Kugel, "On the Bible and Literary Criticism," *Prooftexts* 1 (1981) 224.

[27] M. J. Boda, "Chiasmus in Ubiquity: Symmetrical Mirages in Nehemiah 9," *JSOT* 71 (1996) 55–56. I am paraphrasing in my presentation of Boda's list, and, given the present topic, I have omitted items that pertain only to poetry.

10. A structure should be confirmed by ascertaining its presumed purpose and/or effect.

11. The presupposition that the center of a chiasm is important may be challenged.

While Boda's list is helpful, two items on it are problematic. First, the notion that a "lopsided design" (number 1) is necessarily an error is overly harsh. It appears that in some cases ancient authors varied the lengths of matching features, apparently in order to influence the perceptions of the hearer/reader. For instance, J. C. Exum has pointed out how, in the structure of Judg 13, A′ (v 9) and B′ (v 10) are shorter than are the corresponding A (vv 3–5) and B (vv 6–7), which produces the effect of quickening the pace of the narrative.[28]

Second, Boda too readily dismisses the idea that the center of a chiasm is important (number 11).[29] He cites, on this point, a statement made by D. J. A. Clines: "It would be unwise in our present state of knowledge about Hebrew poetry to conclude that the centre of the strophic structure is also the centre of the thought of the poem."[30] As may be seen, this comment concerns poetry, not narrative, thus reducing its impact in the present case. More important, when Clines makes this remark he is referring to a study by W. Rudolph, in which Rudolph argues for the existence of a psalm in Neh 9:9–37.[31] Rudolph makes no argument for the presence of a chiasm in this passage, however, so, in actuality, Clines' statement is not made in reference to a chiasm. Thus, Boda offers no real reason to reject the importance of the center of a chiastic structure. Further, there are numerous cases where it is clear that the structural center of a chiasm in a narrative setting has special importance. For instance, in Judith the logical center of the text—the beheading of Holofernes—appears at the center of a chiastic structure.[32] Thus, we

[28] See J. C. Exum, "Promise and Fulfillment: Narrative Art in Judges 13," *JBL* 99 (1980) 46 n. 10. Cf. Trible (*Rhetorical Criticism*, 117–19), who asserts that "asymmetry belongs to the warp and woof of symmetry," and discusses the notion of "symmetrophobia" in ancient literature.

[29] Cf. the material concerning Welch's objective criteria of a chiasm in n. 25 above, including a focus or shift at the center. Indeed, the notion that a chiasm features "inversion, balance, and climactic centrality" (Dillard, "The Chronicler's Solomon Narrative," 86) is a widespread claim in the scholarly literature.

[30] D. J. A. Clines, *Ezra, Nehemiah, Esther* (NCB; Grand Rapids, MI: Eerdmans, 1984) 193.

[31] W. Rudolph, *Esra und Nehemia* (Tübingen: J. C. B. Mohr, 1949) 157.

[32] See Craven, *Artistry and Faith*, 62–63.

should at least ask whether, in a given situation, the center of a chiastic structure in a biblical narrative is highlighting some aspect of the material.

As to the overall situation that is reflected in Boda's list, Butterworth makes several observations and suggestions concerning a more appropriate procedure for future studies of structure.[33] To begin with, writers may use repetitions of the same word or root to indicate a correspondence between one part of a text and another. We should be aware, however, that there may be other reasons for such repetition. Above all, repetitions of very common words have little significance in and of themselves. Butterworth holds that repetitions of phrases are likely to be more significant than repetitions of single words, and common words are less likely to be used to indicate structural patterns than are rare and distinctive words.

Further, one should not accept some words as significant, while ignoring others. Instead, what is needed is a systematic approach that examines all possible cases of significant repetition and does not deal with the evidence in an arbitrary fashion. This focus on repeated words does not rule out the possibility that a writer

> might well have had in mind connections between one part and another, progressions of thought, similar type of content, and so forth, which are not reflected in the use of identical words or roots. We may indeed acknowledge that thematic connections such as the above are more important than merely identical words.[34]

[33] Butterworth, *Structure*, 29, 59–61. In what follows, I will summarize Butterworth's comments concerning his methodological stance. I will not attempt to mention all of his points, but merely those that I deem most applicable to the study of narrative works in general, and to the study of 1 Maccabees in particular. It should be noted that Butterworth concentrates on studies of poetic works, but I believe it is reasonable to make use of most of his suggestions in analyzing narrative works as well. Bar-Efrat (*Narrative Art*, 198–99) provides some helpful comments relating to this matter:

> Although it is true that language does not have the same impact in narrative as in poetry, the linguistic design of a narrative is by no means unimportant. While the language of a narrative is not usually as "condensed" as the language of poetry, neither is it as "transparent" as the language of science, for example. Narrative does not use only the basic meanings of words, as science does, but employs their subsidiary meanings too. The language of narrative is distinguished not only from that of science, but also from that of daily speech because, unlike the latter, it is carefully moulded. . . . Consequently, it is appropriate to pay attention to even the minutest details of biblical narratives and to their linguistic features.

[34] Butterworth, *Structure*, 59.

Nevertheless, it has been the case that proposed thematic connections are generally supported in scholarly argumentation by recourse to repeated key words and/or phrases.[35]

Taking these points into consideration, Butterworth outlines a reasonable procedure to use when analyzing biblical texts.

First, establish the divisions of a text independently of structural considerations.

Second, examine all repetitions, and discard those that seem to be insignificant. This step should also be taken without regard to suspected structures.

Third, estimate the likely importance of what remains. Again, the emphasis should be on repetitions of phrases and rare words.

On the basis of these steps, one should be able to uncover the structure of a given text, if it is indeed based—at least in part—on repetition of words and phrases.[36] As a final consideration, Butterworth asserts that one should attempt to explain the purpose(s) of the writer(s)/editor(s) in presenting material in a particular structural fashion.

As I have indicated, in the study to follow I will be adopting Butterworth's methodology. Yet, one further aspect of my method should be mentioned as well. With Butterworth, I consider this study to fall under the general heading of rhetorical criticism. Introductions to rhetorical criticism are readily available and I will therefore keep my comments on the approach to a minimum.[37] I should indicate something of my understanding of the term, however, and the suppositions with which I begin.

[35] Dillard ("The Chronicler's Solomon Narrative," 86) remarks that verbal repetition is given pride of place because it is "the most easily substantiated evidence."

[36] Some reviewers of Butterworth's book mention an experiment performed by him whereby he produces "Isaiah 67" by assembling randomly chosen verses from Isaiah and shows how one could argue that it has a chiastic structure. See Person, review of Butterworth, 134; and R. Mason, *ET* 104 (1993) 247. Yet these reviewers fail to mention how Butterworth (*Structure*, 302) asserts that if he had followed the procedure which he establishes, he would "not have been able to present 'Isaiah 67' as a well-structured whole."

[37] See especially Y. Gitay, "Rhetorical Criticism," *To Each Its Own Meaning: An Introduction to Biblical Criticisms and their Applications* (ed. S. L. McKenzie and S. R. Haynes; Louisville: Westminster/John Knox, 1993) 135–49; A. J. Hauser, "Notes on History and Method," *Rhetorical Criticism of the Bible. A Comprehensive Bibliography with Notes on History and Method* (ed. D. F. Watson and A. J. Hauser; New York: E. J. Brill, 1994) 3–20; and Trible, *Rhetorical Criticism*. See also the following collections of rhetorical-critical articles: *Rhetorical Criticism: Essays in Honor of James Muilenburg* (ed. J. J. Jackson and M. Kessler; PTMS 1; Pittsburgh: Pickwick, 1974), and *Art and Meaning: Rhetoric in Biblical Literature* (ed. D. J. A. Clines et al.; JSOTSup 19; Sheffield: Sheffield Academic, 1982).

Rhetorical criticism of the Hebrew Bible (and its cognate works) received its call to arms in the presidential address given by J. Muilenburg at the 1968 annual meeting of the Society of Biblical Literature.[38] In his address, Muilenburg, while paying tribute to form critics, made the argument that a tendency had arisen in form-critical circles to stress typical and conventional features of a text, and individual and unique features had therefore become shrouded. The exploration of these particularities he dubbed rhetorical criticism, and he stressed that this approach should handle form and content together as a whole. Muilenburg identified two main concerns for the rhetorical critic.[39] The first is to define the limits of a literary unit, while the second is to recognize the structure of a text and to discern the configuration of its component parts. Essentially, as A. J. Hauser remarks, "rhetorical critics are interested in studying the literary features which tie a textual unit together and focus its message."[40]

In keeping with Muilenburg's position, the rhetorical critic's initial concern is to identify the boundaries of a discourse unit. Ancient authors often used formal rhetorical devices to indicate beginnings and endings of units. For instance, occasionally wording at or near the beginning of a unit is repeated or paraphrased at or near the end, thus framing or enveloping the unit. Such an occurrence may be termed an inclusio.[41] Once unit boundaries have been identified by means of the formal rhetorical devices at work, the rhetorical critic may turn to Muilenburg's second concern and analyze questions of structure in and/or among various units.

I should make it clear that, while I will perform a rhetorical-critical investigation in the following pages, I will not attempt to provide a rhetorical "close reading" of 1 Maccabees by dealing with all of the book's rhetorical features on a line-by-line basis. While I will take note of various rhetorical matters, my emphasis is on the overall structure of the book, and not on its texture. S. Bar-Efrat explains:

> Texture is structure looked at through a magnifying glass. It consists of the small-scale relations among the subordinate and generally proximate parts

[38] J. Muilenburg, "Form Criticism and Beyond," *JBL* 88 (1969) 1–18. A collection of Muilenburg's rhetorical-critical studies may be found in *Hearing and Speaking the Word: Selections from the Works of James Muilenburg* (ed. T. F. Best; Chico, CA: Scholars, 1984) 27–255.

[39] Muilenburg, "Form Criticism and Beyond," 8–10.

[40] Hauser, "Notes on History and Method," 8.

[41] See Muilenburg, "Form Criticism and Beyond," 9–10. For a recent discussion of the use of the inclusio in biblical literature, see J. R. Lundbom, "The Inclusio and Other Framing Devices in Deuteronomy I–XXVIII," *VT* 46 (1996) 296–315.

of the narrative, whereas structure proper consists of the relatively large-scale relations among the main and possibly distant parts. Structural analysis, even if it is based on words or phrases, does not usually concern itself with texture. . . .[42]

The Plan of this Study

I am now in a position to outline the remainder of my study. It may be observed in what follows that I will adhere to the principles of rhetorical criticism just discussed as well as to Butterworth's suggested procedure for analyzing the structure of biblical texts.

In chapter two I will identify fundamental literary units of 1 Maccabees.

In chapter three I will examine repetitions in these units.

In chapter four I will attempt to isolate the structure of 1 Maccabees, given the findings of the previous two chapters. I will argue that 1 Maccabees contains three major sections, the first two of which appear to be chiastic structures.

In chapter five I will explore formal symmetries between paired components of the proposed chiastic structures, and will claim that these symmetries confirm the existence of the chiasms.

In chapter six I will take up the major themes that are highlighted in the chiastic structures.

In chapter seven I will deal with the third major section.

I will conclude the study in chapter eight by comparing my view of the structure of 1 Maccabees with alternative theories.[43]

[42] Bar-Efrat, "Analysis of Structure," 158.

[43] I should alert the reader concerning my somewhat limited use of the secondary literature on 1 Maccabees in what follows. In general, I agree with the assessment of Goldstein (*I Maccabees*, xi), who refers to Grimm, Abel, and Bickerman as the "giants of the field." Yet, since my inquiry will largely consist of an immanent study of 1 Maccabees, their works, and those of several other scholars, offer only limited help. In addition, as I noted above, the commentaries on 1 Maccabees concentrate on matters relating to historical issues and literary concerns receive much less attention.

CHAPTER 2

The Literary Units of 1 Maccabees

In this chapter I will separate 1 Maccabees into literary units, so that any structuring of the book established by means of these units may be assessed. Martola has provided a convenient starting point, by assembling pertinent information from some major commentaries. He lists the divisions of 1 Maccabees that occur in the works of C. Grimm, E. Kautzsch, W. Oesterley, H. Bévenot, F.-M. Abel, J. Dancy, J. Nelis, and J. Goldstein.[1] All eight commentators agree that new units begin at the following points: 1:1; 2:1; 3:1, 27; 4:36; 5:1; 6:1; 7:1; 8:1; 9:1, 23; 10:1, 67; 11:1, 20, 38; 12:1; 13:1; 14:1; 15:1; and 16:11.[2] I will argue that new units begin as well at 1:11, 16; 6:18; and 12:24.

In what follows I will isolate various markers of unit boundaries, as well as relevant rhetorical features that shape units. Of primary importance as boundary markers are major shifts in the temporal and/or spatial setting, and in the cast of characters and/or the dramatic situation.[3] It is important to note that the unit boundaries presented in this chapter may have to be

[1] Martola, *Capture and Liberation*, 25–27. For bibliographic information on these commentaries, see nn. 3, 4, 16, 18 in chapter one above.

[2] Each scholar also accepts some additional unit boundaries, but it will prove helpful to focus our attention on those boundaries which are held in common.

[3] These items are standard in the scholarly literature. See, e.g., the discussions in Y. Amit, "Judges 4: Its Contents and Form," *JSOT* 39 (1987) 90; Bar-Efrat, *Narrative Art*, 93–140; E. R. Wendland, "Structural Symmetry and Its Significance in the Book of Ruth," *Issues in Bible Translation* (ed. P. C. Stine; London: United Bible Society, 1988) 31; and Trible, *Rhetorical Criticism*, 123–24.

adjusted at a later point in my investigation, due to structural considerations, since "the limits of [a] literary unit cannot be fixed a priori, but...are dynamic and vary according to the kind of questions the literary critic desires to pose, provided of course that the delimiting of the unit has its justification in the text."[4]

1:1–10

The beginning of this unit is self-evident. The ending is set, in part, by the clear new beginning that takes place in 1:11, which I will discuss below. The contours of the unit are marked additionally by an impressive number of verbal parallels between the opening and closing verses of the unit: (1) the verb ἐξῆλθεν is used in 1:1 and 1:10; (2) the word "earth" appears in 1:1, 2 and 1:9; (3) the phrase καὶ ἐβασίλευσεν is used in 1:1 and 1:10; (4) there is a similarity between the word "Greece" in 1:1 and the word "Greeks" in 1:10; (5) the adjective "many" appears in 1:2 and 1:9; and (6) the word "king" appears in 1:1–2 and 1:10 (and the related word "kingdom" also appears in 1:10). The following highlights these parallels.

> καὶ ἐγένετο μετὰ τὸ πατάξαι Ἀλέξανδρον τὸν Φιλίππου τὸν Μακεδόνα, ὃς <u>ἐξῆλθεν</u> ἐκ τῆς <u>γῆς</u> Χεττιιμ, καὶ ἐπάταξε τὸν Δαρεῖον <u>βασιλέα</u> Περσῶν καὶ Μήδων <u>καὶ ἐβασίλευσεν</u> ἀντ' αὐτοῦ πρότερον ἐπὶ τὴν <u>Ἑλλάδα</u> καὶ συνεστήσατο πολέμους <u>πολλοὺς</u> καὶ ἐκράτησεν ὀχυρωμάτων καὶ ἔσφαξε <u>βασιλεῖς</u> τῆς <u>γῆς</u> (1:1–2)

> After Alexander son of Philip, the Macedonian, who came from the land of Kittim, had defeated King Darius of the Persians and the Medes, he succeeded him as king. (He had previously become king of Greece.) He fought many battles, conquered strongholds, and put to death the kings of the earth.

[4] Bar-Efrat, "Analysis of Structure," 155. Trible (*Rhetorical Criticism*, 103) observes that, "like a building, an individual text has an overall design and numerous sections. . . . The two interrelate. . . . Sometimes you may think you have identified a section only to see it differently in the context of the whole design." One important issue to bear in mind is that "repetition cannot only mark a unit but also indicate secondary material" (T. C. Eskenazi, "The Structure of Ezra-Nehemiah and the Integrity of the Book," *JBL* 107 [1988] 646). Thus, in this chapter I may isolate some apparent unit boundaries and decide at a later point in the investigation that they mark not separate units, after all, but secondary material within units.

> καὶ ἐπέθεντο πάντες διαδήματα μετὰ τὸ ἀποθανεῖν αὐτὸν καὶ οἱ υἱοὶ αὐτῶν ὀπίσω αὐτῶν ἔτη πολλὰ καὶ ἐπλήθυναν κακὰ ἐν τῇ γῇ καὶ ἐξῆλθεν ἐξ αὐτῶν ῥίζα ἁμαρτωλὸς Ἀντίοχος Ἐπιφανὴς υἱὸς Ἀντιόχου τοῦ βασιλέως, ὃς ἦν ὅμηρα ἐν Ῥώμῃ, καὶ ἐβασίλευσεν ἐν ἔτει ἑκατοστῷ καὶ τριακοστῷ καὶ ἑβδόμῳ βασιλείας Ἑλλήνων (1:9–10)

> They all put on crowns after his [sc. Alexander's] death, and so did their descendants after them for many years; and they caused many evils on the earth. From them came forth a sinful root, Antiochus Epiphanes, son of King Antiochus; he had been a hostage in Rome. He began to reign in the one hundred thirty-seventh year of the kingdom of the Greeks.

1:11–15

As I pointed out above, I am adding this unit to the list of those units which are agreed upon by all eight commentators surveyed by Martola. I may note, however, that 1:11–15 is considered a separate unit by four of the eight: Grimm, Dancy, Nelis, and Goldstein.[5] I have already stated that 1:11 makes a clear new beginning. The reasons are that the verse opens with a temporal statement ("In those days . . .") and there is a noticeable change in the cast of characters. While 1:1–10 is dominated by Greek kings, in 1:11–15 we are told about the actions of certain Jewish renegades (υἱοὶ παράνομοι).

There is an interesting framing of the unit. In 1:11 we are told that the renegades wanted to make a covenant with the Gentiles, and in 1:15 we learn that they abandoned the holy covenant and joined with the Gentiles.

> In those days certain renegades came out from Israel and misled many, saying, "Let us go and make a covenant (διαθήκην) with the Gentiles around us, for since we separated from them many disasters have come upon us." (1:11)

> [They] removed the marks of circumcision, and abandoned the holy covenant (διαθήκης ἁγίας). They joined with the Gentiles and sold themselves to do evil. (1:15)

Beyond the repetition of the word διαθήκη, two additional, conceptual features tie 1:11 and 1:15 together. First, the renegades (or lawless ones) of 1:11 are balanced in 1:15 by the phrase: "[they] abandoned the holy covenant."

[5] Grimm, *Das erste Buch der Maccabäer,* 12; Dancy, *A Commentary on I Maccabees,* 58; Nelis, *1 Makkabeeën,* 48; and Goldstein, *I Maccabees,* 199.

Second, in 1:11 the renegades want to "go and make a covenant with the Gentiles around us," which is fulfilled in 1:15 by the statement: "They joined with the Gentiles."

1:16–64

As was the case with the previous unit, I am adding 1:16–64 to the list of units which are agreed upon by all eight commentators, though it should be noted that six of the eight do view 1:16 as a new beginning.[6] The primary reason for considering 1:16 as a unit boundary is that a new course of events commences with this verse, which opens with a subject change as we return to Antiochus IV: "When Antiochus saw that his kingdom was established, he determined to become king of the land of Egypt, in order that he might reign over both kingdoms."

Martola seems to suggest that laments which appear in 1:25–28 and 1:36–40 refer in each case to the events that have just been narrated in the text.[7] The facts, however, do not support such a view. In 1:20–24a Antiochus enters the temple and steals several important ritual objects. We do have a lament following, 1:24b–28, but it does not refer to any robbery, or to ritual objects. Instead, it states that "he shed much blood and spoke with great arrogance," and that Israel therefore mourned and was "clothed with shame." According to 1:29–35 Antiochus sent "a chief collector of tribute" to Jerusalem who fortified the city of David in order to construct a citadel for the Greeks, which the text refers to as a "great menace."[8] The lament that follows, 1:36–40, does appear to refer to the citadel becoming "an evil adversary of Israel," but it also seems to concentrate on the sanctuary: "On every side of the sanctuary they shed innocent blood; they even defiled the sanctuary . . . [the] sanctuary became desolate like a desert."

I would like to suggest, therefore, an alternative explanation of the use of

[6] Grimm, *Das erste Buch der Maccabäer*, 14; Oesterley, "The First Book of Maccabees," 68; Abel, *Les Livres des Maccabées*, 8; Dancy, *A Commentary on I Maccabees*, 63; Nelis, *1 Makkabeeën*, 52; and Goldstein, *I Maccabees*, 202.

[7] See Martola, *Capture and Liberation*, 155, 199.

[8] The name of the "chief collector of tribute" is not given in 1 Maccabees, but it is common to identify him as Apollonius, on the basis of 2 Macc 5:24. On the apparent mistranslation from Hebrew in 1 Macc 1:29 which produces "chief collector of tribute" and not "captain of the Mysians" as in 2 Macc 5:24, see Tedesche and Zeitlin, *The First Book of Maccabees*, 33.

the laments. It seems that the unit 1:16–64 is organized along the following lines.[9]

Introduction (1:16–19)

Episode: the temple is robbed (1:20–24)

Lament (1:25–28)

Episode: the citadel is occupied (1:29–35)

Lament (1:36–40)

Episode: the cult is prohibited (1:41–63)

Summary evaluation (1:64)

In such a structure, the laments function as dividers between episodes and thus they need not refer specifically to the events just narrated in the text.[10]

2:1–70

In 2:1 we have a recurrence of the words used to open 1:11 ("In those days . . ."). We may also observe other signs of a new beginning in 2:1. In addition to the temporal shift, there is a spatial shift, as well as a new cast of characters (Mattathias and his sons). Mattathias' home town of Modein (Μωδεϊν) is mentioned in 2:1, 15, 23, 70.[11] It should be noted that the town name appears in the first and last verses of the unit. Modein appears for the first time in 1 Macc at 2:1 and is not mentioned again after 2:70 until 9:19.

The unit begins with a description of Mattathias and his sons (2:1–5), which is followed by another lament (2:7–13). Mattathias and his sons mourn the recent events in 2:14. Mattathias' zeal in leading a rebellion against Antiochus' measures is recounted in 2:15–28. In 2:29–38 an alternative method of passive resistance is described, which ends in failure when a thousand pious

[9] Bar-Efrat ("Analysis of Structure," 159) provides a similar analysis of 1 Sam 1–2:11.

[10] Dancy (*A Commentary on I Maccabees*, 68, 73) suggests that the lament in 1:25–28 "helps to separate the events of 169 [i.e., Antiochus' temple robbery in 1:21–24] from those of 167 [i.e., the establishment of the citadel in 1:33–35]," and the lament in 1:36–40 "again partly helps to mark the passage of time."

[11] Modein is usually identified with modern Ras Medieh. See F.-M. Abel, *Géographie de la Palestine* (2 vols.; Paris: Gabalda, 1967) 2. 391.

persons die. After a passage about armed resistance (2:39–48), Mattathias gives a farewell address (2:49–68), and then his death and burial are reported (2:69–70). Thus, it can be seen that the figure of Mattathias serves to unite the various components of the unit.[12]

3:1–26

The initial verse of this unit shows clear signs of a new beginning: "Then [Mattathias'] son Judas, who was called Maccabeus, took command in his place." There is, therefore, a shift of attention from Mattathias to Judas and a subject change that accompanies this shift.

We may also note the following framing devices. In 3:6 we read: "Lawbreakers shrank back for fear of [Judas] (ἀπὸ τοῦ φόβου αὐτοῦ)." Similarly, 3:25 states: "Then Judas and his brothers began to be feared (καὶ ἤρξατο ὁ φόβος Ἰούδου καὶ τῶν ἀδελφῶν αὐτοῦ)." The repeated use of "fear" (φόβος) is striking, since the word only appears four times in 1 Maccabees, the other two occasions being 7:18 and 10:8. As we will see, 3:6 and 3:25 are the only times in the book when the word appears more than once in the same unit. In addition, the second verse of the unit (3:2) mentions that "all his brothers (οἱ ἀδελφοὶ αὐτοῦ)" helped Judas, while, as we have just observed, the next to the last verse of the unit states that "Judas and his brothers (τῶν ἀδελφῶν αὐτοῦ) began to be feared" (3:25). These are the first two appearances of the expression "his brothers" in 1 Maccabees.

3:27–4:35

The opening verse of this unit contains a temporal phrase: "When King Antiochus heard these reports, he was greatly angered" (3:27). In addition to the temporal shift, we may also observe a subject change from the preceding unit, which centered on the military successes of Judas.

In 3:34 Antiochus IV gives half his forces to Lysias, the guardian of his young son, and in 3:35 he commands Lysias to annihilate the Jews. This order of extirpation is reflected throughout the rest of the unit. Let us review the pertinent passages.

[12] Cf. Martola, *Capture and Liberation*, 158.

In 3:39 Lysias gathers an army "to go into the land of Judea and destroy it, as the king had commanded."

Afterwards, Judas and his brothers hear that an army has been sent against them. We are told in 3:42 that they "also learned what the king had commanded to do to the people to cause their final destruction."

In 3:46–54 the Jews assemble at Mizpah to prepare themselves for battle.[13] At one point, they cry out: "Here the Gentiles are assembled against us to destroy us" (3:52).

The next day, in a speech to his soldiers before battle, Judas tells them: "Be ready early in the morning to fight with these Gentiles who have assembled against us to destroy us and our sanctuary" (3:58).

The order is mentioned directly only once in 1 Maccabees 4. In 4:27 Lysias is discouraged after hearing a report of how the Jews had defeated his forces. We are told that things had not happened as he had intended, "nor had they turned out as the king had ordered." Nevertheless, even though the order is mentioned only briefly in 1 Maccabees 4, it does play a significant structural role in the chapter, since the threat of annihilation forces the Jews to take measures to prepare to face the Greeks (cf. 4:1–27).[14]

In addition to the material involving Antiochus' order that helps to unite the unit, we may also note the following framing device. In 3:39 Lysias sends some forces "into Judea (εἰς γῆν Ἰούδα)." At the close of the unit Lysias plans "to invade Judea again (πάλιν . . . εἰς τὴν Ἰουδαίαν)" (4:35).

4:36–61

In this unit Judas and his brothers liberate the temple and purify it. The signs of a new beginning in 4:36 are clear. The previous unit, which involves armed conflict, ended with Lysias; and the present unit opens with Judas, his

[13] The location of Mizpah, which was an ancient holy site (see Judg 20:1; 1 Sam 7:6; and 2 Kgs 25:23), has been debated. The major proposals are: (1) Nebi Samwil, a mount approximately eight kilometers northwest of Jerusalem (see, e.g., Grimm, *Das erste Buch der Maccabäer*, 61); and (2) Tell en-Nasbeh, a mound some twelve kilometers north of Jerusalem (see, e.g., Abel, *Les Livres des Maccabées*, 68). Recently, P. M. Arnold ("Mizpah," *ABD* 4. 880) has argued that the archaeological evidence strongly supports the identification with Tell en-Nasbeh.

[14] Cf. Martola, *Capture and Liberation*, 149.

brothers, and their army. This unit involves righteous Jews only, hence there is no warfare. In sum, there is a subject change, a shift in the spatial setting, and a new course of events.

I may also point out some rhetorical devices that structure this unit. First, certain verbs which are used in the opening sentence recur in the body of the unit and divide it into three sections.[15] In 4:36 we read: "Then Judas and his brothers said, 'See, our enemies are crushed; let us go up to cleanse the sanctuary and dedicate it' (ἀναβῶμεν καθαρίσαι τὰ ἅγια καὶ ἐγκαινίσαι)." Our focus will be on the three words: "let us go up (ἀναβῶμεν)"; "to cleanse (καθαρίσαι)"; and "to dedicate (ἐγκαινίσαι)."

In 4:37 we are told that "all the army assembled and went up to Mount Zion (καὶ ἀνέβησαν εἰς ὄρος Σιων)," thus repeating the verb ἀναβαίνω. During the purification of the temple, we first read in 4:41 that "Judas detailed men to fight against those in the citadel until he had cleansed the sanctuary (ἕως καθαρίσῃ τὰ ἅγια)," and then later, in 4:43, we are told: "and they cleansed the sanctuary (καὶ ἐκαθάρισαν τὰ ἅγια)." We observe, then, two occurrences of the word καθαρίζω.

Finally, in 4:54 we read that "at the very season and on the very day that the Gentiles had profaned it, [the altar] was dedicated (ἐνεκαινίσθη) with songs and harps and lutes and cymbals," thus repeating ἐγκαινίζω.

A second structuring device in this unit is an inclusio. In 4:37, as we have seen, the Jewish forces assemble and go up to Mount Zion (ὄρος Σιων). At the end of the unit, in 4:60, they fortify Mount Zion (ὄρος Σιων). These are the first two occurrences of the term ὄρος Σιων in 1 Maccabees.

5:1–68

1 Maccabees 5 begins with a subject change, a spatial shift, and a new course of events. In 5:1 "the Gentiles all around" hear about the temple having been purified and dedicated. As a result, they desire to take vengeance on the Jews who live among them, and indeed, in the words of 5:2, they "kill and destroy among the people." The major part of the chapter then recounts how Judas and his brothers come to the rescue of the threatened Jews and eventually bring many of them to Jerusalem.

[15] Cf. Abel, *Les Livres des Maccabées*, 81, and Martola, *Capture and Liberation*, 116–17, 145.

One feature that helps to tie the unit together is the repetitiveness of the following descriptions of the activities of Judas.[16]

> Then Judas and his army quickly turned back by the wilderness road to Bozrah; and *he took the town*, and *killed every male by the edge of the sword*; then *he seized all its spoils* and *burned it with fire*. (5:28)
>
> Next [Judas] turned aside to Maapha, and fought against it and *took it*; and *he killed every male* in it, *plundered it*, and *burned it with fire*. (5:35)
>
> [Judas] *destroyed every male* [in Ephron] *by the edge of the sword*, and razed and *plundered the town*. Then he passed through the town over the bodies of the dead. (5:51)

Another feature helps to demarcate the boundaries of the unit. In order to facilitate my discussion of this matter we must first survey the contents of the unit. There are five main components: (1) 5:1–2, which serves as an introduction; (2) 5:9–20, in which Judas learns of the predicament facing the Jews in surrounding lands and makes plans for counterattacks; (3) 5:21–23, in which Simon defeats Gentiles in Galilee; (4) 5:24–54, which tells of some successful battles fought by Judas and Jonathan in other surrounding lands; and (5) 5:55–64, which relates an episode concerning Joseph and Azariah. In 5:18 these men are placed in charge of Judea by Judas before he and his brothers leave to face the Gentiles, and in 5:19 they are told specifically by Judas: "Take charge of [the] people, but do not engage in battle with the Gentiles until we return." Nevertheless, having heard of the successes of Judas and his brothers, Joseph and Azariah seek to make a name for themselves too and, going against Judas' express instructions, wage war on some Gentile forces close to Jerusalem (5:58–59). The Gentiles soundly defeat them (5:60). In 5:61 we have a summation of this event that underscores the leadership of the Hasmoneans: "Thus the people suffered a great rout because, thinking to do a brave deed, they did not listen to Judas and his brothers."

Two other stories in 1 Maccabees 5 seem to fall outside of the string of events presented by the five main components.[17] In 5:3–8 Judas leads campaigns against various groups, including the "sons of Esau," and in 5:65–68 he embarks on new expeditions that once more involve attacking the "sons of Esau." We should notice that these stories appear at, or very close to, the beginning and the end of the unit. In addition, these are the only appearances

[16] Cf. Doran, *The First Book of Maccabees*, 78.

[17] Cf. Martola, *Capture and Liberation*, 139–42.

in 1 Maccabees of the term "Esau" (Ησαυ). It would appear, then, that we have another instance of framing. This view is strengthened by observing the intricacies of repetition which appear in the two stories, including the fact that they conclude in the same manner, with Judas returning to Judea/Judah. In the following I have highlighted the repeated material in the two stories.

καὶ ἐπολέμει Ιουδας πρὸς τοὺς υἱοὺς Ησαυ ἐν τῇ Ιδουμαίᾳ τὴν Ακραβαττήνην ὅτι περιεκάθηντο τὸν Ισραηλ καὶ ἐπάταξεν αὐτοὺς πληγὴν μεγάλην καὶ συνέστειλεν αὐτοὺς καὶ ἔλαβεν τὰ σκῦλα αὐτῶν καὶ ἐμνήσθη τῆς κακίας υἱῶν Βαιαν οἳ ἦσαν τῷ λαῷ εἰς παγίδα καὶ σκάνδαλον ἐν τῷ ἐνεδρεύειν αὐτοὺς ἐν ταῖς ὁδοῖς καὶ συνεκλείσθησαν ὑπ' αὐτοῦ εἰς τοὺς πύργους καὶ παρενέβαλεν ἐπ' αὐτοὺς καὶ ἀνεθεμάτισεν αὐτοὺς καὶ ἐνεπύρισε τοὺς πύργους αὐτῆς ἐν πυρὶ σὺν πᾶσιν τοῖς ἐνοῦσιν καὶ διεπέρασεν ἐπὶ τοὺς υἱοὺς Αμμων καὶ εὗρεν χεῖρα κραταιὰν καὶ λαὸν πολὺν καὶ Τιμόθεον ἡγούμενον αὐτῶν καὶ συνῆψεν πρὸς αὐτοὺς πολέμους πολλούς καὶ συνετρίβησαν πρὸ προσώπου αὐτοῦ καὶ ἐπάταξεν αὐτούς καὶ προκατελάβετο τὴν Ιαζηρ καὶ τὰς θυγατέρας αὐτῆς καὶ ἀνέστρεψεν εἰς τὴν Ιουδαίαν (5:3–8)

But Judas made war on the descendants of Esau in Idumea, at Akrabattene, because they kept lying in wait for Israel. He dealt them a heavy blow and humbled them and despoiled them. He also remembered the wickedness of the sons of Baean, who were a trap and a snare to the people and ambushed them on the highways. They were shut up by him in their towers; and he encamped against them, vowed their complete destruction, and burned with fire their towers and all who were in them. Then he crossed over to attack the Ammonites, where he found a strong band and many people, with Timothy as their leader. He engaged in many battles with them, and they were crushed before him; he struck them down. He also took Jazer and its villages; then he returned to Judea.

καὶ ἐξῆλθεν Ιουδας καὶ οἱ ἀδελφοὶ αὐτοῦ καὶ ἐπολέμουν τοὺς υἱοὺς Ησαυ ἐν τῇ γῇ τῇ πρὸς νότον καὶ ἐπάταξεν τὴν Χεβρων καὶ τὰς θυγατέρας αὐτῆς καὶ καθεῖλεν τὰ ὀχυρώματα αὐτῆς καὶ τοὺς πύργους αὐτῆς ἐνεπύρισεν κυκλόθεν καὶ ἀπῆρεν τοῦ πορευθῆναι εἰς γῆν ἀλλοφύλων καὶ διεπορεύετο τὴν Μαρισαν ἐν τῇ ἡμέρᾳ ἐκείνῃ ἔπεσον ἱερεῖς ἐν πολέμῳ βουλόμενοι ἀνδραγαθῆσαι ἐν τῷ αὐτοὺς ἐξελθεῖν εἰς πόλεμον ἀβουλεύτως καὶ ἐξέκλινεν Ιουδας εἰς Ἄζωτον γῆν ἀλλοφύλων καὶ καθεῖλεν τοὺς βωμοὺς αὐτῶν καὶ τὰ γλυπτὰ τῶν θεῶν αὐτῶν κατέκαυσεν πυρὶ καὶ ἐσκύλευσεν τὰ σκῦλα τῶν πόλεων καὶ ἐπέστρεψεν εἰς γῆν Ιουδα (5:65–68)

> Then Judas and his brothers went out and fought the descendants of Esau in the land to the south. He struck Hebron and its villages and tore down its strongholds and burned its towers on all sides. Then he marched off to go into the land of the Philistines, and passed through Marisa. On that day some priests, who wished to do a brave deed, fell in battle, for they went out to battle unwisely. But Judas turned aside to Azotus in the land of the Philistines; he tore down their altars, and the carved images of their gods he burned with fire; he plundered the towns and returned to the land of Judah.

The reader will readily spot the impressive amount of repetition in these passages, but one item is worthy of special notice, and that is the use in each passage of the word θυγατήρ to represent "villages." These are the only such uses in 1 Maccabees. Elsewhere (9:37; 10:54, 57, 58; 11:9, 10, 12) the word appears with its usual meaning of "daughter."

6:1–17

In this unit the focus shifts back to Antiochus IV. The opening words are: "King Antiochus was going through the upper provinces when he heard that. . . ." We may observe a subject change, a spatial shift, and a new course of events, which culminates with the death of the king at 6:16.

The unit is framed. The opening verse, 6:1, contains the words "King Antiochus (ὁ βασιλεὺς Ἀντίοχος)." In the next to last verse, 6:16, we again find the words "King Antiochus," but they are written this time as Ἀντίοχος ὁ βασιλεὺς (a chiastic inclusio). These are the only two occasions in 6:1–17 when Antiochus IV is referred to as "King Antiochus."

In addition, we may observe how the unit is united by means of repetitions of the word λύπη ("grief" or "disappointment"). This word appears four times in 1 Maccabees, all within this unit, and each time with reference to Antiochus IV.[18]

> So he fled and in great disappointment (λύπης μεγάλης) left there to return to Babylon. (6:4)

> When the king heard this news, he was astounded and badly shaken. He took to his bed and became sick from disappointment (λύπης), because things had not turned out for him as he had planned. (6:8)

[18] The word appears forty-five times in the LXX. Thus, the four appearances of the word in this unit in 1 Maccabees represent nearly 9% of the total number of usages in the LXX.

> He lay there for many days, because deep disappointment (λύπη μεγάλη) continually gripped him, and he realized that he was dying. (6:9)
>
> I know that it is because of this that these misfortunes have come upon me; here I am, perishing of bitter disappointment (λύπη μεγάλη) in a strange land. (6:13)

Thus, the narrative literally piles grief upon grief onto Antiochus IV in this unit, which gives the impression of providing a cathartic release: Antiochus IV dies in great anguish, after realizing the error of his ways in how he treated the Jews (cf. 6:12–13).[19]

6:18–63

I am adding this unit to our list, but in this case only one commentator rejects 6:18 as beginning a new unit: Bévenot holds that the unit begins with 6:17, when the young boy, Antiochus V, succeeds his father.[20] I agree with the other seven commentators that 6:18 makes a better beginning, since it offers a subject change, a spatial shift, and a description of a new set of events: "Meanwhile the garrison in the citadel kept hemming Israel in around the sanctuary [and they] were trying in every way to harm them and strengthen the Gentiles."

The unit may be divided into four components: (1) in 6:18–20 Judas besieges the citadel; (2) in 6:21–27 some of the citadel's garrison escapes and, together with "some of the ungodly Israelites," they go to Antiochus and report to him what is happening; (3) in 6:28–54 the king takes military action against Judas and the Jews; and (4) in 6:55–63 the king is told by his guardian, Lysias, that Philip, one of his father's Friends,[21] is trying to seize control of the government, so he quickly makes an offer of peace to the Jews and returns to Antioch.

[19] For further discussion of the rhetorical features of this unit, see my article, "Narrative Art in 1 Maccabees VI 1–17," *VT* 49 (1999) 109–18. In this study I demonstrate that suffering is but part of a larger literary pattern in the unit, since Antiochus' death process contains elements of reversal and recognition as well. I also discuss how this pattern of reversal and recognition accompanied by suffering resonates with Aristotle's discussion of the complex plot in *Poetics* 10–11.

[20] Bévenot, *Die Beiden Makkabäerbücher*, 89.

[21] On the term "Friends" (of the king), see above, chapter one, n. 17.

While the return of Antiochus and Lysias to Antioch possibly suggests an ending, it is not as clearly marked as in the previous units in the book, and may simply represent the limit of secondary material (such as when Judas returns to Judea in 5:8). For the sake of clarity, let us review the boundary markers that we have observed to this point.

- 1:1–10 is framed by various similarities between 1:1–2 and 1:9–10, including repetitions of ἐξῆλθεν, ἐβασίλευσεν, γῆ, and πολύς, while βασιλέα, βασιλεῖς, and Ἑλλάδα in 1:1–2 are reflected by βασιλέως, βασιλείας, and Ἑλλήνων in 1:10

- 1:11–15 is framed by the use of the word διαθήκη, as well as by conceptual correspondences: "lawless ones"(1:11) /"they abandoned the holy covenant (διαθήκης ἁγίας)" (1:15) and "Let us go and make a covenant (διαθήκην) with the Gentiles around us" (1:11)/"They joined with the Gentiles" (1:15)

- 1:16–64 is structured through the alternation of episodes and laments

- 2:1–70 is tied together by the figure of Mattathias and is framed by an inclusio using the place-name Μωδεϊν

- 3:1–26 is framed by repetitions of (1) the word φόβος and (2) the words ἀδελφός and αὐτός

- 3:27–4:35 is united by references to the order by Antiochus IV to extirpate the Jews and is framed by the phrases εἰς γῆν Ἰούδα/πάλιν . . . εἰς τὴν Ἰουδαίαν

- 4:36–61 is structured by repetitions of three verbs (ἀναβαίνω–καθαρίζω–ἐγκαινίζω) and is framed by an inclusio using the words ὄρος Σιων

- 5:1–68 is framed by stories near the beginning and end of the unit which involve campaigns against the υἱοὺς Ησαυ

- 6:1–17 is framed by the words ὁ βασιλεὺς Ἀντίοχος/Ἀντίοχος ὁ βασιλεὺς and is united through the use of the word λύπη

I will suggest immediately below that there is a similar pattern at work throughout 6:18–7:50. Since 6:18–63 lacks a clear ending boundary, such as we have seen in the previous units, we should be alert to the possibility that 6:18 inaugurates a unit that does not end until 7:50.

7:1–50

In 7:1 there is a new character, a temporal shift, a spatial shift, and a new set of events: "In the one hundred fifty-first year Demetrius [I] son of Seleucus [IV] set out from Rome, sailed with a few men to a town by the sea, and there began to reign." Still, as I have just indicated, 6:18–7:50 presents a patterned series of events: three times a Jewish party complains to a king about Judas and the king attempts to punish Judas and his followers. In 6:21–27 it is "some of the ungodly Israelites" who complain to Antiochus V, who then marches against the Jews, accompanied by Lysias (6:28–63). In 7:5–7 "all the lawless and godless men of Israel," led by Alcimus, complain to Demetrius I, who sends his general, Bacchides, against the Jews (7:8–20). In 7:25 Alcimus himself complains to Demetrius, who this time sends Nicanor (7:26–50). Despite the signals of a new beginning in 7:1, the persistence of this pattern throughout 6:18–7:50 suggests that 6:18–63 may be closely tied to 7:1–50.[22]

8:1–32

In 8:1–32 we encounter a shift of focus to Rome: in 8:1–16 a history of the Romans is presented, and in 8:17–32 Judas sends ambassadors to Rome to effect a treaty between the Jews and the Romans.[23] There is, then, a clear change in the cast of characters. In addition, the unit interrupts the flow from 7:1–50 into 9:1–22. In 9:1 we read: "When Demetrius heard that Nicanor and his army had fallen in battle, he sent Bacchides and Alcimus into the land of Judea a second time." This statement, referring to Nicanor's death, hearkens back to 7:43–47, wherein Nicanor is killed by Jews and his body is dismembered.

9:1–22

As we have just seen, 9:1 offers a subject change and a change in the dramatic situation as we leave the Romans and return to the Greeks, who are set

[22] We will explore the specifics of the pattern further in chapter four below.

[23] It is generally accepted that this mission is historical. See, e.g., J.-D. Gauger, *Beiträge zur jüdischen Apologetik* (Cologne/Bonn: Hanstein, 1977) 168–77.

to invade Judea once more. Thus, the beginning of this unit is well marked. In 9:18 Judas is killed in battle. I noted in chapter one that, in the *communis opinio*, a major part of 1 Maccabees ends shortly thereafter, at 9:22. I will have more to say on this topic immediately below.

9:23–73

While the commentators view this material as constituting a separate unit, there are difficulties with this position. First, 9:1–57 provides a connected account of a military expedition and is, as Martola puts it, "a rounded whole."[24] Second, the figure of Bacchides unites 1 Maccabees 9. In 9:1 Demetrius I sends Bacchides to Judea. In 9:11–18 Bacchides' forces face and kill Judas. Then, in 9:32, Bacchides also tries to kill Jonathan, who has taken over as leader of the Hasmonean cause. In 9:43–53, however, Bacchides loses in battle against Jonathan, and then retreats and establishes some fortifications. When he learns that Alcimus is dead, Bacchides returns to his own land, and there is peace for two years (9:57). In 9:58–60 some "lawless" Jews successfully entice Bacchides to return, but in 9:72 he leaves for good.

In sum, the evidence suggests that 9:1–22 is closely tied to 9:23–73. We should therefore be alert to the possibility that 9:22 marks the limit of secondary material and not a unit boundary.

10:1–66

In 10:1 we are introduced to a new person, Alexander Balas, a pretender to the Syrian throne, who claimed to be the son of Antiochus IV. His arrival is accompanied by spatial and temporal shifts: "In the one hundred sixtieth year Alexander Epiphanes, son of Antiochus, landed and occupied Ptolemais." Demetrius I, learning of this new challenger, assembled an army to confront Alexander (10:2) and also tried to obtain good relations with Jonathan and the Jews by means of some friendly letters (10:3–6, 25–45).[25] Alexander tried to counter Demetrius' actions with regard to Jonathan by sending a letter of

[24] Martola, *Capture and Liberation*, 165.

[25] Scholars diverge on the authenticity of the letter in 10:25–45. For example, H. Willrich (*Urkundenfälschung in der hellenistisch-jüdischen Literatur* [Göttingen: Vandenhoeck & Ruprecht, 1924] 37–41) thinks it is a forgery, while Goldstein (*I Maccabees*, 405) considers it reliable.

his own (10:17–20) in which he appointed Jonathan high priest and named him a Friend.

The reader is struck by the new status of Jonathan in this material. He is now, as Martola remarks, one of the "mighty ones in the Seleucid Empire."[26] Due to the rivalry between Alexander Balas and Demetrius I (who dies in battle at 10:50), Jonathan's position is greatly enhanced as the two royal claimants outdo one another in attempting to curry favor with him. Eventually, some Jewish opponents attempt to harass Jonathan, but they are soundly rebuked by Alexander and flee (10:61–64). The king then elevates Jonathan's standing by having Jonathan seated at his side, clothed in purple (10:62–63). Further still, Alexander has his officers accompany Jonathan into the middle of Ptolemais where they "proclaim that no one is to bring any charges against him about any matter" (10:63).

10:67–89

10:67 provides a strong new beginning with a subject change, as well as temporal and spatial shifts: "In the one hundred sixty-fifth year Demetrius [II] son of Demetrius [I] came from Crete to the land of his ancestors." According to 10:69 Demetrius appointed Apollonius the governor of Coelesyria to challenge Jonathan, and Apollonius assembled a large force with which to do so. Jonathan and Simon were able to withstand the attack, however, and were ultimately victorious over Apollonius' forces (10:74–87).

There is an apparent framing of this unit. In the second verse of the unit we are told: "When King Alexander [Balas] heard (καὶ ἤκουσεν Ἀλέξανδρος ὁ βασιλεὺς) of [the emergence of Demetrius II] he was greatly distressed" (10:68). The next to the last verse of the unit records: "When King Alexander heard (καὶ ἐγένετο ὡς ἤκουσεν Ἀλέξανδρος ὁ βασιλεὺς) of [the successful Jewish expedition against Apollonius], he honored Jonathan still more" (10:88).

11:1–19

11:1 suggests a new beginning, since it features a subject change, a spatial shift, and a new dramatic situation: "Then the king of Egypt [Ptolemy VI] gathered great forces . . . and he tried to get possession of Alexander's king-

[26] Martola, *Capture and Liberation*, 169.

dom by trickery." This unit is largely concerned with the enmity between Alexander Balas and Ptolemy VI, as well as the struggle for the Seleucid throne between Alexander and Demetrius II. Ptolemy and Alexander eventually meet in battle (11:15). Alexander then goes to Arabia, where he is killed (11:17). Ptolemy, however, did not live much longer himself (11:18). 11:19 concludes: "So Demetrius became king."

11:20–37

11:20 reads as follows: "In those days Jonathan assembled the Judeans to attack the citadel in Jersualem, and he built many engines of war to use against it." Thus, the verse suggests another beginning, since there is a new dramatic situation, accompanied by temporal and spatial shifts. Eventually, Jonathan won the favor of Demetrius II, who exalted Jonathan in the presence of his Friends (11:26). Indeed, according to 11:27, Demetrius "confirmed [Jonathan] in the high priesthood and in as many other honors as he had formerly had, and caused him to be reckoned among his chief Friends." Demetrius also granted the Jews various favors, including tax relief (11:30–37).

11:38–74

11:38 features a new course of events: "When King Demetrius [II] saw that the land was quiet before him and that there was no opposition to him, he dismissed all his troops." The unit is largely concerned with the problems encountered by Demetrius, for he became embattled by the citizenry of Antioch as well as by Trypho, the guardian of the child king Antiochus VI, the young son of Alexander Balas.[27]

12:1–23

In this unit there is a subject change as Jonathan sends a mission to Rome "to confirm and renew the friendship with them" (12:1) and, according to 12:2, he also sent letters to the Spartans and some others.[28] 12:1–23 is

[27] Trypho[n]'s real name was Diodotus. Trypho is an epithet meaning "Magnificent." On this matter, see Grimm, *Das erste Buch der Maccabäer*, 177.

[28] Scholars are not in agreement concerning the authenticity of Jonathan's letter to the

enclosed by two invasions led by officers of Demetrius II. The enclosure, which marks out 12:1–23 as a distinct unit, is made manifest through repetition.

11:63	12:24
καὶ ἤκουσεν Ιωναθαν ὅτι	καὶ ἤκουσεν Ιωναθαν ὅτι
παρῆσαν οἱ ἄρχοντες Δημητρίου	ἐπέστρεψαν οἱ ἄρχοντες Δημητρίου
εἰς Κεδες τὴν ἐν τῇ Γαλιλαίᾳ	
μετὰ δυνάμεως πολλῆς	μετὰ δυνάμεως πολλῆς ὑπὲρ τὸ πρότερον
βουλόμενοι μεταστῆσαι αὐτὸν τῆς χρείας	τοῦ πολεμῆσαι πρὸς αὐτόν
Then Jonathan heard that	Now Jonathan heard that
the officers of Demetrius	the commanders of Demetrius
had come	had returned,
to Kadesh in Galilee	
with a large army,	with a larger force than before,
intending to remove him from office.	to wage war against him.

12:24–53

This is the last of the four units that I add to our list. 12:23 provides a good ending, since it closes a document, and 12:24, which we have just seen, is a good beginning, with a subject change, an implied spatial shift, and a description of a new dramatic situation. Six of the eight commentators examined by Martola hold that 12:24 supplies a new beginning.[29]

In 12:24–38 we read about: (1) campaigns by Jonathan against the forces of Demetrius II (12:24–30) and "the Arabs who are called Zabadeans" (12:31–32); (2) a campaign by Simon (12:33–34); and (3) a report of fortifications put up by the two brothers (12:35–38). Then, in 12:39–53, attention turns back to the struggle for the Syrian crown. Trypho, who covets the

---

Spartans. Abel (*Les Livres des Maccabées*, 231–33), for instance, defends it, while several others, such as B. Cardauns ("Juden und Spartaner," *Hermes* 95 [1967] 320–21), express doubts.

[29] Grimm, *Das erste Buch der Maccabäer*, 191; Bévenot, *Die Beiden Makkabäerbücher*, 142; Abel, *Les Livres des Maccabées*, 224; Dancy, *A Commentary on I Maccabees*, 168; Nelis, *1 Makkabeeën*, 215; and Goldstein, *I Maccabees*, 463.

throne, plans to murder Antiochus VI as well as Jonathan (12:39–40). Trypho is able to get Jonathan to come to Ptolemais, where the Jewish leader is seized (12:41–48). In 12:49–53 Jews mourn because they fear that Jonathan is dead.

13:1–53

In this unit Simon comes to the fore. It begins with a subject change and an implied spatial change: "Simon heard that Trypho had assembled a large army to invade the land of Judea and destroy it" (13:1). In 13:2–10 Simon encourages the Jews who support the Hasmonean cause, which rekindles them to the point that they ask him to become their leader, and he assembles warriors and fortifies Jerusalem. We learn that surprisingly Jonathan is still alive, however, and Trypho offers to release him for a hundred talents of silver, plus the surrender of two hostages (13:14–16). Even though Simon complies with the demands, Trypho murders Jonathan (13:23). Simon and his followers mourn again, and Simon buries his brother at the family tomb (13:25–30). Meanwhile, Trypho kills the young Antiochus VI and names himself king (13:31–32). Simon makes an overture to Demetrius II, who agrees to a "general peace" with the Jews (13:34–42). Simon then takes Gazara (13:43–48), and also liberates and purifies the citadel (13:49–50). The day that the Jews enter the citadel is deemed a festive occasion, "because a great enemy had been crushed and removed from Israel" (13:51). Therefore Simon declares that the day should be celebrated annually (13:52).

14:1–49

14:1 provides a temporal shift, a spatial shift, and a description of a new dramatic situation: "In the one hundred seventy-second year King Demetrius [II] assembled his forces and marched into Media to obtain help, so that he could make war against Trypho." The march east of Demetrius ends in failure when he is seized by one of the generals of King Arsaces of Persia and Media (14:2–3). 14:4–15 then presents a poem summarizing Simon's career. As we saw in chapter one above, Martola believes that the first edition of 1 Maccabees ended with this poem. Indeed, in the past many scholars felt that the book had originally ended at this point. I will return to this topic in chapter seven below. It is interesting to note now, though, that at 14:16 we seemingly have a new beginning: there is a spatial shift and a description of a new course of events. The verse reads: "It was heard in Rome, and as far away as Sparta, that Jonathan had died, and they were deeply grieved." Six of the eight commentators Martola surveys consider 14:16 to be a new beginning.[30]

Much of the remainder of the unit is taken up by a popular decree in honor of Simon (14:27–45) that is said to be issued by "the great assembly of priests and the people and the rulers of the nation and the elders of the country" (14:28).

15:1–16:10

In 15:1 we find a change in the cast of characters and a spatial shift: "Antiochus [VII], son of King Demetrius [I], sent a letter from the islands of the sea to Simon." Antiochus, who is preparing to fight Trypho, confirms the freedom of the Jews in his letter (15:2–9). Thereafter, he sets out against Trypho, who flees from before him to the city of Dor, which Antiochus surrounds (15:10–14). Simon sends two thousand troops to assist Antiochus, but Antiochus rebuffs him, breaks "all the agreements he formerly had made with Simon," and becomes "estranged from him" (15:26–27).[31] Antiochus then sends one of his Friends, Athenobius, to demand the return of certain cities, as well as the citadel, but Simon refuses, which greatly angers Antiochus (15:28–36). Next, Trypho escapes the siege (15:37), and Antiochus sends an army, led by Cendebeus, against Simon (15:38–41). Simon, now an old man, turns the leadership over to his sons Judas and John (Hyrcanus), and they defeat the Syrian force (16:1–10).[32]

16:11–24

This unit begins with a change in the cast of characters, a spatial shift, and a new course of events:

[30] Grimm, *Das erste Buch der Maccabäer*, 210; Oesterley, "The First Book of Maccabees," 118; Bévenot, *Die Beiden Makkabäerbücher*, 155; Abel, *Les Livres des Maccabées*, 252; Dancy, *A Commentary on I Maccabees*, 182; and Nelis, *1 Makkabeeën*, 233.

[31] In 15:15–24 a delegation returns to Jerusalem from Rome after renewing the friendship and alliance established earlier (cf. 8:17–32 and 12:1–4). According to the text, they carry a letter on behalf of the Jews by Lucius, the Roman consul. Scholars are divided on the authenticity of this letter. On this matter, see Sievers, *The Hasmoneans*, 117–18. Some scholars have suggested that 15:15–24 are displaced and belong somewhere before 14:25. See, e.g., Goldstein, *I Maccabees*, 493–94.

[32] On the leadership of the Jews at 16:4, see n. 10 in chapter seven below.

> Now Ptolemy son of Arubus had been appointed governor over the plain of Jericho; he had a large store of silver and gold, for he was son-in-law of the high priest. His heart was lifted up; he determined to get control of the country, and made treacherous plans against Simon and his sons, to do away with them (16:11–13).

Ptolemy assassinated Simon and his two sons Mattathias and Judas (16:14–17), and sought to murder the third son, John, as well (16:19). John was told, however, what had happened to his father and brothers, and was warned that men were after him too (16:21). Thus forewarned, he was able to seize the men who came to destroy him and have them killed (16:22). The story ends at that point, bringing the unit—and the book—to a close (16:23–24).

Conclusion

In this chapter we have reviewed the primary literary units in 1 Maccabees, guided by some major commentaries. The unit boundaries between 1:1 and 6:17 are clearly marked by rhetorical features. The units after this point, however, often lack clear boundary markers. Thus, some of the unit boundaries for the material following 6:17 may need to be reevaluated at a later point in my investigation.

In the following chapter I will identify instances of key repetitions in 1 Maccabees, in order to isolate those which might serve to link separate literary units.

CHAPTER 3

Repetitions of Rare Words in 1 Maccabees

My approach in this chapter is based on the method proposed by Butterworth, which I discussed in chapter one. In order to eliminate subjectivity, I will examine various repetitions in the literary units of 1 Maccabees without regard to any suspected structure of the book. The reader will recall that Butterworth recommends examining all repetitions, discarding those which seem to be insignificant, and estimating the likely importance of those that remain. Such a procedure may have merit in the investigation of short texts, where every word might have some significance. It would be onerous, however, in dealing with a book as long as 1 Maccabees. In keeping with Butterworth's opinion that common words are less likely to be used to mark structure than distinctive words, I will concentrate on rare words, which I define for the present purposes as those which appear in 1 Maccabees between two and five times and, at the same time, in the LXX less than 75 times.[1] Thus, such words are not only rare in 1 Maccabees, but are also (relatively) rare in the Bible as a whole.[2]

[1] It should be noted that, although Butterworth recommends examining every repetition, his actual practice is akin to the procedure I will follow in this chapter. In his book, Butterworth studies both the structure of individual literary units in Zechariah as well as connections between units. While he does examine every repetition *within* individual units, when he turns to consider possible connections *between* units he restricts his attention to distinctive words. Butterworth (*Structure*, 238) explains: "It is obvious that a word which would mark out a structure in one connected section would not necessarily be effective over a longer distance, especially when material of a different kind intervenes between two occurrences."

[2] Of course, as Bar-Efrat (*Narrative Art*, 199) points out, "Since we are unaware of the full

Taking note as well of Butterworth's suggestion that repetitions of phrases are likely to be more significant than repetitions of single words, I will investigate the usages in 1 Maccabees of the rare words in repeated phrases. In an effort to achieve clarity, consistency, and objectivity, my approach is mechanical: if two or more separate words (including at least one rare word) are used consecutively in the same sequence in at least two literary units in 1 Maccabees, I will regard the sequence as a repeated phrase.[3]

I should point out that the majority of the uses of the rare words in 1 Maccabees include no repeated phrases. Further, it should be clear that the repetitions listed in the following pages do not exhaust the usages in 1 Maccabees of the rare words involved. These are merely the instances that appear in repeated phrases in at least two units.

Three items in my approach should now be clarified. First, by the term "word" I mean a dictionary form and do not require that the phrases involve the same morphology. Second, since the Greek of 1 Maccabees is translated from Hebrew, I will require that a sequence of two separate words in the Greek text reflect what would also be at least two separate words in Hebrew for the words to count as a phrase, or as part of a phrase. For instance, the sequence in Greek of καί plus a verb will not count as a phrase, since in Hebrew the conjunction used with the verb would normally be attached directly to the verb. Third, as a counterpoint to the previous consideration, I will not allow material that is separate in Greek but would be attached to a following word in Hebrew, to prohibit consideration of what would otherwise be a repeated phrase. For example, twice in 1 Maccabees the Jews celebrate "with harps and cymbals." Yet, while in 4:54 the Greek has καὶ κινύραις καὶ κυμβάλοις, in 13:51 we find καὶ ἐν κινύραις καὶ ἐν κυμβάλοις. As may be seen, in the second formulation the preposition ἐν appears between καὶ and κινύραις/κυμβάλοις. In Hebrew, however, either formulation would involve only two separate words, since both the conjunction and the preposition (*b*) would be attached directly to the following noun. Thus, we should consider this wording in 4:54 and 13:51 to constitute a repeated phrase.

---

extent and precise nature of the Hebrew language in biblical times (the Bible itself contains a very limited part of the language used at the time) it is impossible to assess accurately the rarity or deviance of any given word or linguistic phenomenon."

3 In keeping with my mechanical approach, when highlighting these phrases below I will simply underline the repeated material whether or not it includes the complete grammatical unit in which the material appears.

In order not to burden the reader, I have eliminated from the following presentation material that appears to offer no help to the present investigation. Instead, I have limited our attention to those words which seem relevant to the task of uncovering the structure of 1 Maccabees. The following has been my guiding principle: mere repetition alone does not necessarily denote any linkage between or among units, and thus some other indication of a connection must be present for any repetition to be considered as possibly being an indicator of structure.[4] Given this consideration, I will be dividing the words listed below into two different categories. First, when a repetition involves similar episodes, it will be considered a *promising* indicator of structure. This step will be taken because the repeated material appears in similar dramatic settings and this suggests sustained similarity. Second, when a repetition displays some sign of linkage other than similar episodes (namely, the same or a similar cast of characters and/or settings) it will be considered a *possible* indicator of structure.[5]

Repetitions

1. ἀνδραγαθία[6]

> <u>καὶ διηγήσαντο αὐτῷ τοὺς πολέμους αὐτῶν καὶ τὰς ἀνδραγαθίας, ἃς ποιοῦσιν</u> ἐν τοῖς Γαλάταις, καὶ ὅτι κατεκράτησαν αὐτῶν καὶ ἤγαγον αὐτοὺς ὑπὸ φόρον (8:2)
>
> [Judas] had been told of their wars and of the brave deeds that [the Romans] were doing among the Gauls, how they had defeated them and forced them to pay tribute.
>
> καὶ τὰ περισσὰ τῶν λόγων Ἰούδου <u>καὶ τῶν πολέμων καὶ τῶν ἀνδρα-</u>

[4] Butterworth (*Structure*, 56) rightly observes: "In any passage several verses long there are bound to be repetitions. Only if a word has some additional distinctive feature can it be taken to be significant."

[5] I have chosen to ignore from the outset all cases where a phrase includes a name, since we should be cautious about the repeated use of technical terms that may occur in a text out of necessity and not from any structural design. Thus, all such cases have been eliminated from what follows. To be sure, by leaving out such material it may be that I have set aside some repetitions that are meaningful for determining structure. My intent in this chapter, however, is not to isolate *all* repetitions that are of possible structural significance, but rather those which can be used with most confidence.

[6] The rare words will be presented in alphabetical order.

γαθιῶν, ὧν ἐποίησε καὶ τῆς μεγαλωσύνης αὐτοῦ οὐ κατεγράφη· πολλὰ γὰρ ἦν σφόδρα (9:22)

Now the rest of the acts of Judas, and his wars and the brave deeds that he did, and his greatness, have not been recorded, but they were very many.

καὶ ἤκουσεν Ἀλέξανδρος ὁ βασιλεὺς τὰς ἐπαγγελίας, ὅσας ἀπέστειλε Δημήτριος τῷ Ιωναθαν, καὶ διηγήσαντο αὐτῷ τοὺς πολέμους καὶ τὰς ἀνδραγαθίας, ἃς ἐποίησεν αὐτὸς καὶ οἱ ἀδελφοὶ αὐτοῦ, καὶ τοὺς κόπους, οὓς ἔσχοσαν (10:15)

Now King Alexander [Balas] heard of all the promises that Demetrius [I] had sent to Jonathan, and he heard of the battles that Jonathan and his brothers had fought, of the brave deeds that they had done, and of the troubles that they had endured.

καὶ τὰ λοιπὰ τῶν λόγων Ιωάννου καὶ τῶν πολέμων αὐτοῦ καὶ τῶν ἀνδραγαθιῶν αὐτοῦ, ὧν ἠνδραγάθησε, καὶ τῆς οἰκοδομῆς τῶν τειχῶν, ὧν ᾠκοδόμησε, καὶ τῶν πράξεων αὐτοῦ (16:23)

The rest of the acts of John [Hyrcanus] and his wars and the brave deeds that he did, and the building of the walls that he completed, and his achievements [are in the annals of his high priesthood].

The wording of these verses displays varying degrees of similarity. Essentially, the verses fall into two groups. The first group is 8:2 and 10:15, each of which employs the rare word διηγέομαι (see 7. below). No connection between these verses is discernible. The second group is 9:22 and 16:23, which lack διηγέομαι. We have already observed the seeming parallel between 9:22 and 16:23–24 in chapter one above and thus we may regard the repetition in these two verses as a possible indicator of structure.

2. ἀσπίς

μετὰ ταῦτα ἀπέστειλε Σίμων τὸν Νουμήνιον εἰς Ῥώμην ἔχοντα ἀσπίδα χρυσῆν μεγάλην ὁλκὴν μνῶν χιλίων εἰς τὸ στῆσαι πρὸς αὐτοὺς τὴν συμμαχίαν (14:24)

After this Simon sent Numenius to Rome with a large gold shield weighing one thousand minas, to confirm the alliance with the Romans.

ἤνεγκαν δὲ ἀσπίδα χρυσῆν ἀπὸ μνῶν χιλίων (15:18)

[Numenius and his companions] have brought a gold shield weighing one thousand minas.

In these verses we find repeated phrases involving two rare words–ἀσπίς and μνᾶ (see 18. below). The verses do exhibit a connection. In 15:18 Lucius, a Roman consul, writes in a letter that the Jewish envoy Numenius, who had been sent to Rome with a large gold shield in 14:24, had arrived. Thus, we should regard the repetition as a possible indicator of structure. Still, we should bear in mind that there "are very few events in biblical narrative which have neither a causal nor a sequential role to play in the chain of the narrative."[7] 15:18 seems to illustrate this point, since it looks like a simple report that the intent of 14:24 had been achieved.

3. ἄφεμα

> καὶ <u>ἀφήσομεν ὑμῖν ἀφέματα</u> πολλὰ καὶ δώσομεν ὑμῖν δόματα (10:28)
>
> We [sc. Demetrius I] will grant you [sc. the Jews] many immunities and give you gifts.
>
> τὸν στέφανον τὸν χρυσοῦν καὶ τὴν βαΐν, ἣν ἀπεστείλατε, κεκομίσμεθα καὶ ἕτοιμοί ἐσμεν τοῦ ποιεῖν ὑμῖν εἰρήνην μεγάλην καὶ γράφειν τοῖς ἐπὶ τῶν χρειῶν τοῦ <u>ἀφιέναι ὑμῖν ἀφέματα</u> (13:37)
>
> We [sc. Demetrius II] have received the gold crown and the palm branch that you [sc. Simon and the Jews] sent, and we are ready to make a general peace with you and to write to our officials to grant you release from tribute.

These phrases appear in letters written by kings named Demetrius. The letters are addressed, however, to slightly different entities. In 10:28 Demetrius I is writing to the Jews (cf. 10:25), and in 13:37 Demetrius II is writing to the Jews and Simon (cf. 13:36). Still, the overall similarity between the verses suggests that I should categorize this repetition as a possible indicator of structure.

4. βουλευτήριον

> καὶ ἐπορεύθησαν εἰς Ῥώμην–καὶ ἡ ὁδὸς πολλὴ σφόδρα–<u>καὶ εἰσήλθοσαν εἰς τὸ βουλευτήριον</u> καὶ ἀπεκρίθησαν καὶ εἶπον (8:19)
>
> [Eupolemus son of John son of Accos and Jason son of Eleazar] went to Rome, a very long journey; and they entered the senate chamber and spoke.

[7] Bar-Efrat, *Narrative Art*, 96.

> καὶ ἐπορεύθησαν εἰς Ῥώμην καὶ εἰσῆλθον εἰς τὸ βουλευτήριον καὶ εἶπαν Ιωναθαν ὁ ἀρχιερεὺς καὶ τὸ ἔθνος τῶν Ἰουδαίων ἀπέστειλεν ἡμᾶς ἀνανεώσασθαι τὴν φιλίαν αὐτοῖς καὶ τὴν συμμαχίαν κατὰ τὸ πρότερον (12:3)
>
> So they [sc. "men" chosen by Jonathan] went to Rome and entered the senate chamber and said, "The high priest Jonathan and the Jewish nation have sent us to renew the former friendship and alliance with them."

The phrase involving βουλευτήριον is surrounded by additional repetitions (the phrases καὶ ἐπορεύθησαν εἰς Ῥώμην and καὶ εἶπον/καὶ εἶπαν appear in each verse). While the subjects of the repeated material differ, the verses appear in similar episodes, in which a Jewish delegation goes to Rome and addresses the Roman senate. A further connection is revealed in 12:3, where we learn that the second delegation was sent to renew the alliance that was established by the first delegation.[8] In sum, this repetition should be categorized as a promising indicator of structure.

5. δέλτος

> καὶ τοῦτο τὸ ἀντίγραφον τῆς ἐπιστολῆς, ἧς ἀντέγραψαν ἐπὶ δέλτοις χαλκαῖς καὶ ἀπέστειλαν εἰς Ιερουσαλημ εἶναι παρ' αὐτοῖς ἐκεῖ μνημόσυνον εἰρήνης καὶ συμμαχίας (8:22)
>
> This is a copy of the letter that [the Romans] wrote in reply, on bronze tablets, and sent to Jerusalem to remain with them there as a memorial of peace and alliance.
>
> ἔγραψαν πρὸς αὐτὸν δέλτοις χαλκαῖς τοῦ ἀνανεώσασθαι πρὸς αὐτὸν φιλίαν καὶ τὴν συμμαχίαν, ἣν ἔστησαν πρὸς Ἰούδαν καὶ Ιωναθαν τοὺς ἀδελφοὺς αὐτοῦ (14:18)
>
> [The Romans and the Spartans] wrote to [Simon] on bronze tablets to renew with him the friendship and alliance that they had established with his brothers Judas and Jonathan.
>
> ἐστήρισε γὰρ αὐτὸς καὶ οἱ ἀδελφοὶ αὐτοῦ καὶ ὁ οἶκος τοῦ πατρὸς αὐτοῦ καὶ ἐπολέμησε τοὺς ἐχθροὺς Ισραηλ ἀπ' αὐτῶν. καὶ ἔστησαν αὐτῷ

[8] Based on her analysis of the technical terms used in the accounts of the delegations sent to Rome in 1 Maccabees, S. R. Mandell ("Did the Maccabees Believe that They Had a Valid Treaty with Rome?" *CBQ* 53 [1991] 218) holds that, in actuality, 1 Maccabees 8 is "clearly a later tradition than 1 Macc 12:1."

ἐλευθερίαν καὶ κατέγραψαν ἐν <u>δέλτοις χαλκαῖς</u> καὶ ἔθεντο ἐν στήλαις ἐν ὄρει Σιων (14:26)

"For [Simon] and his brothers and the house of his father have stood firm; they have fought and repulsed Israel's enemies and established its freedom." So [the Jews] made a record on bronze tablets and put it on pillars on Mount Zion.

καὶ τὴν γραφὴν ταύτην εἶπαν θέσθαι ἐν <u>δέλτοις χαλκαῖς</u> καὶ στῆσαι αὐτὰς ἐν περιβόλῳ τῶν ἁγίων ἐν τόπῳ ἐπισήμῳ (14:48)

And [the Jews] gave orders to inscribe this decree on bronze tablets, to put them up in a conspicuous place in the precincts of the sanctuary.

14:18, 26, 48 all belong to the same literary unit. There is an apparent connection between units in regard to 8:22 and 14:18, however, since the latter verse refers, in part, to matters associated with the former verse, as well as the fact that the verses share similar casts of characters. Thus, the repeated material in these verses should be considered a possible indicator of structure.

6. διαπορεύομαι

καὶ ὁ βασιλεὺς παρέλαβε τὰς ἡμίσεις τῶν δυνάμεων τὰς καταλειφθείσας καὶ ἀπῆρεν ἀπὸ Ἀντιοχείας ἀπὸ πόλεως βασιλείας αὐτοῦ ἔτους ἑβδόμου καὶ τεσσαρακοστοῦ καὶ ἑκατοστοῦ καὶ διεπέρασε τὸν Εὐφράτην ποταμὸν καὶ <u>διεπορεύετο τὰς ἐπάνω χώρας</u> (3:37)

Then the king [sc. Antiochus IV] took the remaining half of his forces and left Antioch his capital in the one hundred and forty- seventh year. He crossed the Euphrates river and went through the upper provinces.

καὶ ὁ βασιλεὺς Ἀντίοχος <u>διεπορεύετο τὰς ἐπάνω χώρας</u> καὶ ἤκουσεν ὅτι ἐστὶν Ἐλυμαῒς ἐν τῇ Περσίδι πόλις ἔνδοξος πλούτῳ, ἀργυρίῳ καὶ χρυσίῳ (6:1)

King Antiochus was going through the upper provinces when he heard that Elymais in Persia was a city famed for its wealth in silver and gold.

We dealt with this repetition in chapter one above, and saw that it is easily explained since 6:1 is the next time that Antiochus IV is mentioned in 1 Maccabees after 3:37 and the repetition thus reintroduces him. Still, since Antiochus appears in each verse, I should categorize the repetition as a possible indicator of structure.

7. διηγέομαι. See 1. above.

8. εἰκάς

> καὶ πέμπτῃ καὶ εἰκάδι τοῦ μηνὸς θυσιάζοντες ἐπὶ τὸν βωμόν, ὃς ἦν ἐπὶ τοῦ θυσιαστηρίου (1:59)
>
> On the twenty-fifth day of the month [the Greeks] offered sacrifice on the altar of burnt offering.
>
> καὶ ὤρθρισαν τὸ πρωῒ τῇ πέμπτῃ καὶ εἰκάδι τοῦ μηνὸς τοῦ ἐνάτου—οὗτος ὁ μὴν Χασελευ—τοῦ ὀγδόου καὶ τεσσαρακοστοῦ καὶ ἑκατοστοῦ ἔτους (4:52)
>
> Early in the morning on the twenty-fifth day of the ninth month, which is the month of Chislev, in the one hundred forty-eighth year [the Jews offered sacrifice on the new altar].

In these verses εἰκάς appears with another rare word, πέμπτος (see 21. below). There is a specific relationship between the two verses since in 4:52–53 the Jews embark on making use of a new altar that they have made to replace the altar which was desecrated by the Greeks in 1:59. Thus, there is an evident similarity to the episodic settings of these two verses, making the repetition a promising indicator of structure.

9. ἐμβατεύω

> καὶ ἀπῆρεν ἐξ Ιερουσαλημ καὶ ἀπήντησεν αὐτοῖς εἰς τὴν Αμαθῖτιν χώραν· οὐ γὰρ ἔδωκεν αὐτοῖς ἀνοχὴν τοῦ ἐμβατεῦσαι εἰς τὴν χώραν αὐτοῦ (12:25)
>
> [Jonathan] marched away from Jerusalem and met them [sc. a force sent by Demetrius II] in the region of Hamath, for he gave them no opportunity to invade his own country.
>
> καὶ μετὰ ταῦτα ἦλθε Τρύφων τοῦ ἐμβατεῦσαι εἰς τὴν χώραν καὶ ἐκτρῖψαι αὐτήν, καὶ ἐκύκλωσαν ὁδὸν τὴν εἰς Αδωρα, καὶ Σιμων καὶ ἡ παρεμβολὴ αὐτοῦ ἀντιπαρῆγεν αὐτῷ εἰς πάντα τόπον, οὗ ἂν ἐπορεύετο (13:20)
>
> After this Trypho came to invade the country and destroy it, and he circled around by the way to Adora. But Simon and his army kept marching along opposite him to every place he went.

καὶ ἐβουλήθησαν οἱ ἐχθροὶ αὐτῶν ἐμβατεῦσαι εἰς τὴν χώραν αὐτῶν τοῦ ἐκτρῖψαι τὴν χώραν αὐτῶν καὶ ἐκτεῖναι χεῖρας ἐπὶ τὰ ἅγια αὐτῶν (14:31)

When their enemies decided to invade their country and lay hands on their sanctuary [Simon rose up and fought for his nation].

Given the differences in the casts of characters and the settings among the verses, there is no evident structural relationship between 12:25 and either 13:20 or 14:31. Since the latter two verses each involve Simon, however, I should categorize the repeated phrase in these verses as a possible indicator of structure. It would seem, though, that the wording manifests military terminology ("to invade a country"), and the repetition is of dubious significance.

10. ἐντυγχάνω

καὶ ἐπισυνήχθησαν ἐπ' αὐτὸν ἄνδρες λοιμοὶ ἐξ Ισραηλ, ἄνδρες παράνομοι, ἐντυχεῖν κατ' αὐτοῦ, καὶ οὐ προσέσχεν αὐτοῖς ὁ βασιλεύς (10:61)

A group of malcontents from Israel, renegades, gathered together against [Jonathan] to accuse him; but the king [sc. Alexander Balas] paid no attention to them.

καὶ ἐκάθισεν αὐτὸν ὁ βασιλεὺς μετ' αὐτοῦ καὶ εἶπε τοῖς ἄρχουσιν αὐτοῦ Ἐξέλθατε μετ' αὐτοῦ εἰς μέσον τῆς πόλεως καὶ κηρύξατε τοῦ μηδένα ἐντυγχάνειν κατ' αὐτοῦ περὶ μηδενὸς πράγματος, καὶ μηδεὶς αὐτῷ παρενοχλείτω περὶ παντὸς λόγου (10:63)

The king [sc. Alexander Balas] also seated [Jonathan] at his side; and he said to his officers, "Go out with him into the middle of the city and proclaim that no one is to bring charges against him about any matter, and let no one annoy him for any reason."

καὶ ἐνετύγχανον κατ' αὐτοῦ τινες ἄνομοι τῶν ἐκ τοῦ ἔθνους (11:25)

Although certain renegades of [Jonathan's] nation kept making complaints against him [Demetrius II treated him as his predecessors had treated him and exalted him].

The collocation of ἐντυγχάνω plus κατ' αὐτοῦ appears only these three times in the LXX. The verses occur in similar episodic settings. In both 10:59–66 and 11:20–37 the same sequence of events transpires. First, a king writes Jonathan to tell him to come to Ptolemais for a meeting. Jonathan then goes to Ptolemais, bearing gifts. He wins the royal favor and, when some of his enemies attempt to slander him, the king ignores them and instead grants Jonathan an exalted position among the king's advisors. Thus, the repeated collocation is surrounded by other parallels in similar episodes, making it a promising indicator of structure.

11. ἐπίσημος

> νῦν οὖν ἐπιμέλεσθε τοῦ ποιῆσαι τούτων ἀντίγραφον, καὶ δοθήτω Ιωναθαν καὶ τεθήτω ἐν τῷ ὄρει τῷ ἁγίῳ <u>ἐν τόπῳ ἐπισήμῳ</u> (11:37)
>
> Now therefore take care to make a copy of this, and let it be given to Jonathan and put up in a conspicuous place on the holy mountain.
>
> καὶ τὴν γραφὴν ταύτην εἶπαν θέσθαι ἐν δέλτοις χαλκαῖς καὶ στῆσαι αὐτὰς ἐν περιβόλῳ τῶν ἁγίων <u>ἐν τόπῳ ἐπισήμῳ</u> (14:48)
>
> And they gave orders to inscribe this decree [concerning Simon] on bronze tablets, to put them up in a conspicuous place in the precincts of the sanctuary.

Though the casts of characters in these verses differ, the settings are similar, in that a copy of an important document involving one of the Hasmonean brothers is placed in "a conspicuous place" on the holy mountain/in the sanctuary precincts. Thus, we should consider this repetition to be a possible indicator of structure, though it should be noted that the procedure of setting up a permanent copy of an important document on stone or metal in a sacred enclosure was not unusual in antiquity.[9]

12. ἐρημόω

> <u>τὸ ἁγίασμα αὐτῆς ἠρημώθη</u> ὡς ἔρημος, αἱ ἑορταὶ αὐτῆς ἐστράφησαν εἰς πένθος, τὰ σάββατα αὐτῆς εἰς ὀνειδισμόν, ἡ τιμὴ αὐτῆς εἰς ἐξουδένωσιν (1:39)
>
> [Jerusalem's] sanctuary became desolate like a desert; her feasts were turned into mourning, her sabbaths into a reproach, her honor into contempt.
>
> καὶ εἶδον <u>τὸ ἁγίασμα ἠρημωμένον</u> καὶ τὸ θυσιαστήριον βεβηλωμένον

[9] See Goldstein, *1 Maccabees*, 366.

καὶ τὰς πύλας κατακεκαυμένας καὶ ἐν ταῖς αὐλαῖς φυτὰ πεφυκότα ὡς ἐν δρυμῷ ἢ ὡς ἐν ἑνὶ τῶν ὀρέων καὶ τὰ παστοφόρια καθῃρημένα (4:38)

There [Judas' army] saw the sanctuary desolate, the altar profaned, and the gates burned. In the courts they saw bushes sprung up as in a thicket, or as on one of the mountains. They saw also the chambers of the priests in ruins.

As may be seen, each verse concerns the sanctuary, which is described as being "desolate." Given this similarity, I should classify the repetition as a possible indicator of structure.

13. εὐοδύω

καὶ ἐν ταῖς ἡμέραις αὐτοῦ εὐοδώθη ἐν ταῖς χερσὶν αὐτοῦ τοῦ ἐξαρθῆναι τὰ ἔθνη ἐκ τῆς χώρας αὐτῶν καὶ τοὺς ἐν τῇ πόλει Δαυιδ τοὺς ἐν Ιερουσαλημ, οἳ ἐποίησαν ἑαυτοῖς ἄκραν, ἐξ ἧς ἐξεπορεύοντο καὶ ἐμίαινον κύκλῳ τῶν ἁγίων καὶ ἐποίουν πληγὴν μεγάλην ἐν τῇ ἁγνείᾳ (14:36)

In [Simon's] days things prospered in his hands, so that the Gentiles were put out of the country, as were also those in the city of David in Jerusalem, who had built themselves a citadel from which they used to sally forth and defile the environs of the sanctuary, doing great damage to its purity.

καὶ ἐκάλεσε Σίμων τοὺς δύο υἱοὺς αὐτοῦ τοὺς πρεσβυτέρους Ἰούδαν καὶ Ιωάννην καὶ εἶπεν αὐτοῖς Ἐγὼ καὶ οἱ ἀδελφοί μου καὶ ὁ οἶκος τοῦ πατρός μου ἐπολεμήσαμεν τοὺς πολεμίους Ισραηλ ἀπὸ νεότητος ἕως τῆς σήμερον ἡμέρας, καὶ εὐοδώθη ἐν ταῖς χερσὶν ἡμῶν ῥύσασθαι τὸν Ισραηλ πλεονάκις (16:2)

And Simon called in his two eldest sons Judas and John, and said to them: "My brothers and I and my father's house have fought the wars of Israel from our youth until this day, and things have prospered in our hands so that we have delivered Israel many times."

The collocation of εὐοδύω plus χείρ appears fourteen times in the LXX, which suggests that it is common language.[10] Even so, since both of these verses involve Simon, I should classify this repetition as a possible indicator of structure.

[10] In addition to the two verses examined above, the collocation appears at Gen 39:3, 23; 1 Kgs 22:12, 15; Dan 8:25; Ezra 5:8; 2 Chr 18:11, 14; 1 Esdr 6:9; 1 Macc 3:6; 2 Macc 10:23; Wis 11:1.

14. καταοικίζω

> καὶ ἐξέβαλεν ἐξ αὐτῆς πᾶσαν ἀκαθαρσίαν καὶ κατῴκισεν ἐν αὐτῇ ἄνδρας, οἵτινες τὸν νόμον ποιοῦσι, καὶ προσωχύρωσεν αὐτὴν καὶ ᾠκοδόμησεν ἑαυτῷ ἐν αὐτῇ οἴκησιν (13:48)
>
> [Simon] removed all uncleanness from [Gazara], and settled in it those who observed the law. He also strengthened its fortifications and built in it a house for himself.
>
> καὶ κατῴκισεν ἐν αὐτῇ ἄνδρας Ἰουδαίους καὶ ὠχύρωσεν αὐτὴν πρὸς ἀσφάλειαν τῆς χώρας καὶ τῆς πόλεως καὶ ὕψωσεν τὰ τείχη Ιερουσαλημ (14:37)
>
> [Simon] settled Jews in [the citadel] and fortified it for the safety of the country and of the city, and built the walls of Jerusalem higher.

There is obviously a similarity between Simon having settled "those who observed the law" in Gazara (13:48) and Jews in the citadel (14:37). Thus, we should consider the repetition to be a possible indicator of structure. These verses appear in consecutive units, however, and therefore they may have merely a sequential relationship.

15. κινύρα

> κατὰ τὸν καιρὸν καὶ κατὰ τὴν ἡμέραν, ἐν ᾗ ἐβεβήλωσαν αὐτὸ τὰ ἔθνη, ἐν ἐκείνῃ ἐνεκαινίσθη ἐν ᾠδαῖς καὶ κιθάραις καὶ κινύραις καὶ κυμβάλοις (4:54)
>
> At the very season and on the very day that the Gentiles had profaned [the altar], it was dedicated with songs and harps and lutes and cymbals.
>
> καὶ εἰσῆλθον εἰς αὐτὴν τῇ τρίτῃ καὶ εἰκάδι τοῦ δευτέρου μηνὸς ἔτους ἑνὸς καὶ ἑβδομηκοστοῦ καὶ ἑκατοστοῦ μετὰ αἰνέσεως καὶ βαΐων καὶ ἐν κινύραις καὶ ἐν κυμβάλοις καὶ ἐν νάβλαις καὶ ἐν ὕμνοις καὶ ἐν ᾠδαῖς, ὅτι συνετρίβη ἐχθρὸς μέγας ἐξ Ισραηλ (13:51)
>
> On the twenty-third day of the second month, in the one hundred seventy-first year, the Jews entered [the citadel] with praise and palm branches, and with harps and cymbals and stringed instruments, and with hymns and songs, because a great enemy had been crushed and removed from Israel.

In these verses κινύρα appears together with another rare word, κύμβαλον (see 17. below). The verses occur in the context of similar episodes. In 4:54, having liberated the temple from the hands of the Greeks, the Jews rededicate the altar; in 13:51 the Jews liberate the citadel. In each case, the Jews mark the moment with traditional music, and they also perform purification rituals (cf. 4:43 and 13:50). The overall similarity of episodic settings makes this a promising repetition.

16. κοίτη

> καὶ μετὰ ταῦτα ἔπεσεν ἐπὶ τὴν κοίτην καὶ ἔγνω ὅτι ἀποθνῄσκει (1:5)
>
> After this [Alexander the Great] fell on the bed and perceived that he was dying.
>
> καὶ ἐγένετο ὡς ἤκουσεν ὁ βασιλεὺς τοὺς λόγους τούτους, ἐθαμβήθη καὶ ἐσαλεύθη σφόδρα καὶ ἔπεσεν ἐπὶ τὴν κοίτην καὶ ἐνέπεσεν εἰς ἀρρωστίαν ἀπὸ τῆς λύπης, ὅτι οὐκ ἐγένετο αὐτῷ καθὼς ἐνεθυμεῖτο (6:8)
>
> When the king [sc. Antiochus IV] heard this news, he was astounded and badly shaken. He fell on the bed and became sick from disappointment, because things had not turned out for him as he had planned.

This is a promising repetition. As we saw in chapter one, in each verse the repeated phrase appears in an episodic setting in which a king (Alexander the Great/Antiochus IV) dies.

17. κύμβαλον. See 15. above.

18. μνᾶ. See 2. above.

19. νῆσος

> καὶ ἀπὸ βασιλειῶν ἑτέρων καὶ ἀπὸ νήσων θαλασσῶν ἦλθον πρὸς αὐτὸν δυνάμεις μισθωταί (6:29)
>
> Mercenary forces also came to [Antiochus V] from other kingdoms and from islands of the seas.
>
> καὶ μετὰ πάσης τῆς δόξης αὐτοῦ ἔλαβε τὴν Ἰόππην εἰς λιμένα καὶ ἐποίησεν εἴσοδον ταῖς νήσοις τῆς θαλάσσης (14:5)
>
> To crown all his honors [Simon] took Joppa for a harbor, and opened a way to the isles of the sea.

καὶ ἀπέστειλεν Ἀντίοχος υἱὸς Δημητρίου τοῦ βασιλέως ἐπιστολὰς ἀπὸ <u>τῶν νήσων τῆς θαλάσσης</u> Σιμωνι ἱερεῖ καὶ ἐθνάρχῃ τῶν Ἰουδαίων καὶ παντὶ τῷ ἔθνει (15:1)

Antiochus [VII], son of King Demetrius, sent a letter from the islands of the sea to Simon, the priest and ethnarch of the Jews, and to all the nation.

There seems to be no structural connection between 6:29 and the other verses. Each of the other two concerns Simon in some way, however, so I should classify the repetition in 14:5 and 15:1 as a possible indicator of structure.

20. παράνομος

καὶ ἔθηκαν ἐκεῖ ἔθνος ἁμαρτωλόν, <u>ἄνδρας παρανόμους,</u> καὶ ἐνίσχυσαν ἐν αὐτῇ (1:34)

[The Greeks] stationed [at the City of David] a sinful people, men who were renegades. These strengthened their position.

καὶ ἐπισυνήχθησαν ἐπ᾽ αὐτὸν ἄνδρες λοιμοὶ ἐξ Ισραηλ, <u>ἄνδρες παράνομοι,</u> ἐντυχεῖν κατ᾽ αὐτοῦ, καὶ οὐ προσέσχεν αὐτοῖς ὁ βασιλεύς (10:61)

A group of malcontents from Israel, renegades, gathered together against [Jonathan] to accuse him; but the king [sc. Alexander Balas] paid no attention to them.

καὶ ἐπορεύθησάν τινες μισοῦντες τὸ ἔθνος αὐτῶν <u>ἄνδρες παράνομοι</u> πρὸς τὸν βασιλέα καὶ ἀπήγγειλαν αὐτῷ ὅτι Ιωναθαν περικάθηται τὴν ἄκραν (11:21)

But certain renegades who hated their nation went to the king [sc. Demetrius II] and reported to him that Jonathan was besieging the citadel.

In each of these verses παράνομος appears with ἀνήρ. 1:34 is not directly related to the other two verses, but it is clear that 10:61 and 11:21 are similar: in each case some renegades go to a king to slander Jonathan. The reader will recall 10:61 from number 10 above. I noted there that in both 10:59–66 and 11:20–37 Jonathan goes to Ptolemais per the request of a king, and, despite attacks from some of his enemies, he wins royal favor. Given the similar episodic settings, this repetition is a promising indicator of structure.

21. πέμπτος. See 8 above.

22. πόρπη

καὶ ἀπέστειλεν αὐτῷ πόρπην χρυσῆν, ὡς ἔθος ἐστὶν δίδοσθαι τοῖς συγγενέσι τῶν βασιλέων, καὶ ἔδωκεν αὐτῷ τὴν Ακκαρων καὶ πάντα τὰ ὅρια αὐτῆς εἰς κληροδοσίαν (10:89)

And [Alexander Balas] sent to [Jonathan] a golden buckle, such as it is the custom to give to the King's Kinsmen. He also gave him Ekron and all its environs as his possession.

καὶ ἀπέστειλεν αὐτῷ χρυσώματα καὶ διακονίαν καὶ ἔδωκεν αὐτῷ ἐξουσίαν πίνειν ἐν χρυσώμασι καὶ εἶναι ἐν πορφύρᾳ καὶ ἔχειν πόρπην χρυσῆν (11:58)

[Antiochus VI] also sent [Jonathan] gold plate and a table service, and granted him the right to drink from gold cups and dress in purple and wear a gold buckle.

καὶ οὐκ ἐξέσται οὐθενὶ τοῦ λαοῦ καὶ τῶν ἱερέων ἀθετῆσαί τι τούτων καὶ ἀντειπεῖν τοῖς ὑπ' αὐτοῦ ῥηθησομένοις καὶ ἐπισυστρέψαι συστροφὴν ἐν τῇ χώρᾳ ἄνευ αὐτοῦ καὶ περιβάλλεσθαι πορφύραν καὶ ἐμπορποῦσθαι πόρπην χρυσῆν (14:44)

None of the people or priests shall be permitted to nullify any of these decisions or to oppose what [Simon] says, or to convene an assembly in the country without his permission, or to be clothed in purple or put on a gold buckle.

14:44 clearly seems unrelated to the other two verses. In both 10:89 and 11:58, however, we find a king giving Jonathan various items, including a gold buckle.[11] This similarity makes the repetition in these two verses a possible indicator of structure.

23. σάκκος

καὶ διέρρηξε Ματταθίας καὶ οἱ υἱοὶ αὐτοῦ τὰ ἱμάτια αὐτῶν καὶ περιεβάλοντο σάκκους καὶ ἐπένθησαν σφόδρα (2:14)

Then Mattathias and his sons tore their clothes, put on sackcloth, and mourned greatly.

[11] On the significance of this buckle, see E. J. Bickerman, *Institutions de Séleucides* (Paris: Geuthner, 1938) 43.

καὶ ἐνήστευσαν τῇ ἡμέρᾳ ἐκείνῃ καὶ περιεβάλοντο σάκκους καὶ σποδὸν ἐπὶ τὴν κεφαλὴν αὐτῶν καὶ διέρρηξαν τὰ ἱμάτια αὐτῶν (3:47)

[The Jews] fasted that day, put on sackcloth and sprinkled ashes on their heads, and tore their clothes.

Though the casts of characters differ somewhat in these two verses, there is sufficient commonality–both putting on of sackcloth and tearing of clothes by faithful Jews–to classify this repetition as a possible indicator of structure. We should note, however, that, being traditional customs, neither action is rare in the Bible, even in combination.[12]

24. ὑφίστημι

πῶς δυνησόμεθα ὑποστῆναι κατὰ πρόσωπον αὐτῶν, ἐὰν μὴ σὺ βοηθήσῃς ἡμῖν; (3:53)

How will we [sc. the Jews] be able to withstand them, if you [sc. God] do not help us?

καὶ εἶπε Τιμόθεος τοῖς ἄρχουσι τῆς δυνάμεως αὐτοῦ ἐν τῷ ἐγγίζειν Ἰούδαν καὶ τὴν παρεμβολὴν αὐτοῦ ἐπὶ τὸν χειμάρρουν τοῦ ὕδατος ἐὰν διαβῇ πρὸς ἡμᾶς πρότερος, οὐ δυνησόμεθα ὑποστῆναι αὐτόν, ὅτι δυνάμενος δυνήσεται πρὸς ἡμᾶς (5:40)

Now as Judas and his army drew near to the stream of water, Timothy said to the officers of his forces, "If he crosses over to us first, we will not be able to resist him, for he will surely defeat us."

ὡς δὲ εἶδεν Ἄλκιμος ὅτι ἐνίσχυσεν Ἰούδας καὶ οἱ μετ' αὐτοῦ, καὶ ἔγνω ὅτι οὐ δύναται ὑποστῆναι αὐτούς, καὶ ἐπέστρεψε πρὸς τὸν βασιλέα καὶ κατηγόρησεν αὐτῶν πονηρά (7:25)

When Alcimus saw that Judas and those with him had grown strong, and realized that he could not withstand them, he returned to the king [sc. Antiochus V] and brought malicious charges against them.

καὶ νῦν οὐ δυνήσῃ ὑποστῆναι τὴν ἵππον καὶ δύναμιν τοιαύτην ἐν τῷ πεδίῳ, ὅπου οὐκ ἔστι λίθος οὐδὲ κόχλαξ οὐδὲ τόπος τοῦ φυγεῖν (10:73)

And now you [sc. Jonathan] will not be able to withstand my [sc. Apollonius'] cavalry and such an army in the plain, where there is no stone or pebble, or place to flee.

[12] The following are some examples where the two activities are mentioned in the same verse: Gen 37:34; 2 Sam 3:31; 2 Kgs 19:1; Esth 4:1.

The collocation of ὑφίστημι plus δύναμαι appears in each of these verses. This collocation is rare in the LXX, appearing in only one other place (Josh 7:12). Judas is mentioned in both 5:40 and 7:25, and thus the repetition in these verses should be deemed a possible indicator of structure.

25. χαρά

> καὶ ἔστησεν Ἰούδας καὶ οἱ ἀδελφοὶ αὐτοῦ καὶ πᾶσα ἡ ἐκκλησία Ισραηλ ἵνα ἄγωνται αἱ ἡμέραι τοῦ ἐγκαινισμοῦ τοῦ θυσιαστηρίου ἐν τοῖς καιροῖς αὐτῶν ἐνιαυτὸν κατ' ἐνιαυτὸν ἡμέρας ὀκτὼ ἀπὸ τῆς πέμπτης καὶ εἰκάδος τοῦ μηνὸς Χασελευ μετ' εὐφροσύνης καὶ χαρᾶς (4:59)
>
> Then Judas and his brothers and all the assembly of Israel determined that every year at that season the days of dedication of the altar should be observed with joy and gladness for eight days, beginning with the twenty-fifth day of the month of Chislev.
>
> καὶ ἀνέβησαν εἰς ὄρος Σιων ἐν εὐφροσύνῃ καὶ χαρᾷ καὶ προσήγαγον ὁλοκαυτώματα, ὅτι οὐκ ἔπεσεν ἐξ αὐτῶν οὐθεὶς ἕως τοῦ ἐπιστρέψαι ἐν εἰρήνῃ (5:54)
>
> So they [sc. Judas and "the people"] went up to Mount Zion with joy and gladness, and offered burnt offerings, because they had returned in safety; not one of them had fallen.

As may be seen, the casts of characters in these two verses are similar, and, since Judas is involved in each case, I will identify the repetition as a possible indicator of structure. We should note, however, that the settings of the verses are quite different. In 4:59 the people have "joy and gladness" because they have liberated the temple. In 5:54 they have "joy and gladness" because they have returned safely from various military campaigns.

Conclusion

In this chapter I have examined repetitions of several rare words that may be helpful in identifying the structure of 1 Maccabees. Eight of the words that were examined were deemed to be promising indicators of structure. They are: βουλευτήριον (4); εἰκάς (8); ἐντυγχάνω (10); κινύρα (15); κοίτη (16); κύμβαλον (17); παράνομος (20); and πέμπτος (21). I classified sixteen words as being possible indicators of structure. They are: ἀνδραγαθία (1); ἀσπίς (2); ἄφεμα (3); δέλτος (5); διαπορεύομαι (6); ἐμβατεύω (9); ἐπίσημος (11);

ἐρημόω (12); εὐοδόω (13); κατοικίζω (14); μνᾶ (18); νῆσος (19); πόρπη (22); σάκκος (23); ὑφίστημι (24); and χαρά (25). In the following chapter I will use these words to guide us into the architecture of 1 Maccabees.[13]

[13] By the term "architecture" I mean that which Trible (*Rhetorical Criticism*, 107–122) and Craven (*Artistry and Faith*, 47–64) call "external design," and what J. C. Exum ("Aspects of Symmetry and Balance in the Samson Saga," *JSOT* 19 [1981] 9–10) refers to as "structural design," which she explains as "the skeleton upon which the narrative is fashioned."

CHAPTER 4

The Architecture of 1 Maccabees

In the following pages I will focus on the words that were identified as promising indicators of structure in the previous chapter. I will also incorporate words that were deemed possible structural indicators where appropriate. Let us begin by observing that the eight words which were identified as promising indicators appear in five seemingly paired sets of episodes.[1]

(1) βουλευτήριον
Jewish mission to Rome (8:17–32)
Jewish mission to Rome (12:1–4)

(2) εἰκάς and πέμπτος
desecration of the altar (1:20–24, 54–59)
dedication of a new altar (4:51–56)

(3) ἐντυγχάνω and παράνομος
Jonathan visits Ptolemais (10:59–66)
Jonathan visits Ptolemais (11:20–37)

(4) κινύρα and κύμβαλον[2]
liberation of the temple (4:36–59)
liberation of the citadel (13:49–51)

[1] In the following, I am once more arranging according to the alphabetical order of the Greek words.

[2] The dedication of a new altar in number 2 above, which takes place at 4:51–56, also appears within the context of the liberation of the temple (4:36–59).

(5) κοίτη
  Alexander the Great dies (1:5–7)
  Antiochus IV dies (6:8–16)

I will set aside the liberation episodes (number 4) for the time being, and will return to them in chapter six below. The other four pairs present some striking patterns when their distribution in literary units (as identified in chapter two above) is considered.

Pattern Number One

1:1–10	Alexander the Great dies
1:16–64	desecration of the altar
4:36–61	dedication of a new altar
6:1–17	Antiochus IV dies

Pattern Number Two

8:1–32	Jewish mission to Rome
10:1–66	Jonathan visits Ptolemais
11:20–37	Jonathan visits Ptolemais
12:1–23	Jewish mission to Rome

We may observe in these patterns skeletal outlines of two possible chiastic structures, since in each case the outer and inner units are paired, at least in part.

There are some compelling reasons to investigate this matter further. As to pattern number one, we have already observed in chapter one above some parallels between the sequences of events when Alexander the Great and Antiochus IV die. In addition, the episode of the dedication of a new altar has much in common with the episode of the desecration of the original altar (cf. 1:59 and 4:52–53). Of course, this similarity is not necessarily surprising.

> Dramatic narratives ordinarily have a "bell curve" contour: they proceed from the aperture and staging through several episodes which build up the tension in the narrative to that moment of "peak" tension at which denouement is begun; the denouement winds down ordinarily through several episodes which unravel the tension generated by the pre-peak build-up, and finally concludes with an epilogue or postscript. Narratives having such a

> bell curve must have a certain degree of parallelism: the issues which caused the tension must be resolved in the second half of the story, i.e., a certain amount of repetition is inevitable. Due to the inherent repetition such dramatic narratives could easily be metanalyzed incorrectly as chiastic.[3]

Still, we may observe the emphatic note struck in 4:54 that the new altar was dedicated "at the very season and on the very day that the Gentiles had profaned it." This remark ties the two events together in an especially forceful way. In any case, the possibility of a chiasm should be investigated, since the dying king episodes may be artificially linked given the fact that there are numerous ways to describe the deaths of different individuals which do not necessitate substantial repetition.

Turning to pattern number two, its pairs of episodes have drawn the attention of some scholars. For instance, concerning the diplomatic missions to Rome in 8:17–32 and 12:1–4, Martola comments: "The similarities between the accounts both in vocabulary and the order between the clauses are so great and numerous that they quite evidently form a scheme."[4] With regard to Jonathan's visits to Ptolemais to meet with royalty, Dancy writes that the first visit (10:59–66) is "a scene which bears many resemblances [to the second visit, 11:20–37]."[5]

In sum, there is sufficient evidence to prompt an investigation of possible chiastic structures in 1 Maccabees, along the lines suggested by the two patterns above.[6] I will investigate these possible structures separately. I will refer to the first possible chiastic structure (suggested by pattern number one) as "section one." I will refer to the second possible chiastic structure (suggested by pattern number two) as "section two."

Section One

If all of the literary units that were identified in chapter two above from 1:1 to 6:17 are set out, in conjunction with pattern number one, a chiastic struc-

[3] Dillard, "The Chronicler's Solomon Narrative," 86–87. Cf. T. Longman III, *Literary Approaches to Biblical Interpretation* (Grand Rapids, MI: Zondervan, 1987) 102.

[4] Martola, *Capture and Liberation*, 229.

[5] Dancy, *A Commentary on I Maccabees*, 156.

[6] Cf. Dillard ("The Chronicler's Solomon Narrative," 86), who suggests that "[w]here repetition is frequent . . . the analyst must at least ask if the narrative has been constructed with a chiastic architecture."

ture emerges. Chiasms are typically presented with capital letters representing various features and corresponding letters with a prime (′) to indicate matching (inverted) features. By following this practice, the structure may be summarized as follows.

A 1:1–10 Alexander the Great dies
  B 1:11–15
    C 1:16–64 desecration of the altar
      D 2:1–70
        E 3:1–26
      D′ 3:27–4:35
    C′ 4:36–61 dedication of a new altar
  B′ 5:1–68
A′ 6:1–17 Antiochus IV dies

As may be seen, this arrangement aligns the two pairs of episodes listed under pattern number one above: AA′, wherein first Alexander the Great and then Antiochus IV die; and CC′, in which the altar is desecrated by the Greeks and a new altar is dedicated by the Jews. I may add that one of the words deemed to be a possible indicator of structure in the previous chapter, ἐρημόω, supports the linkage of CC′.

There are further similarities between the matching units in this chiastic arrangement. First, in BB′ local Gentiles figure prominently, as the opening verses of the units suggest.

> In those days certain renegades came out from Israel and misled many, saying, "Let us go and make a covenant with the Gentiles around us (τῶν ἐθνῶν τῶν κύκλῳ ἡμῶν). . . ." (1:11)

> When the Gentiles all around (τὰ ἔθνη κυκλόθεν) heard that the altar had been rebuilt . . . they became very angry, and they determined to destroy the descendants of Jacob who lived among them. So they began to kill and destroy among the people. (5:1–2)

Second, in DD′ contrasting instructions are given. In D Mattathias directs his sons to revolt against the Greeks (2:67–68), while in D′ Antiochus IV orders Lysias to attack those Jews who have revolted against him (3:35–36). In addition, another word that was categorized as a possible indicator of structure in the previous chapter, σάκκος, supports a linkage between D and D′.

Thus, a reasonable argument can be made for exploring the possibility that section one has a chiastic structure. Further evidence will be sought in the following chapter to allow us to accept or to reject the possible chiasm.

Section Two

The situation is more complicated with regard to section two. Let us begin by reviewing what we saw in pattern number two: 8:1–32 and 12:1–23 feature comparable episodes (Jewish missions to Rome) that use similar phrases containing βουλευτήριον, while 10:1–66 and 11:20–37 contain comparable episodes (visits by Jonathan to Ptolemais) that use similar phrases containing the words ἐντυγχάνω and παράνομος. Each of these pairs of episodes appears to be connected in some way. Yet if the literary units from 8:1–32 to 12:1–23 that were identified in chapter two above are arranged, as I have done with the units in section one, we find that this time one of the pairs of episodes does not align.

A 8:1–32 Jewish mission to Rome
  B 9:1–22
    C 9:23–73
      D 10:1–66 Jonathan visits Ptolemais
        E 10:67–89
      D′ 11:1–19
    C′ 11:20–37 Jonathan visits Ptolemais
  B′ 11:38–74
A′ 12:1–23 Jewish mission to Rome

As may be seen, while AA′ does pair up the missions to Rome, Jonathan's visits do not match, since they appear in D and C′.

Our first impulse, given this result, might be to drop the matter of section two entirely, and to rule out the possibility of any chiastic structure past 6:17. The reader will recall from my survey in chapter two, however, that, with some exceptions, the boundaries of the various literary units after 6:1–17 are not as clearly marked by rhetorical devices as are the units from 1:1–10 to 6:1–17. Several explanations for this phenomenon are possible: (1) for some reason, the author(s) became less interested in using such devices after 6:17; (2) the material becomes more complex (for instance, there is only one king from 1:1–10 to 6:1–17 [Antiochus IV] but several royal figures in the latter part of the book) making it more difficult for the author(s) to control the material; or (3) perhaps we have not correctly identified all of the units following 6:1–17. As to the last possibility, we saw in chapter two above that some of the unit boundaries after 6:17 were problematic. Bearing this matter in mind, I would like to reconsider the following units: 9:1–22, 23–73; 10:1–66, 67–89; and 11:1–19, 20–37, 38–74.

In chapter two I noted that, while scholars generally see an ending at 9:22, following Judas' death, 9:1–57 actually provides a connected account of a military campaign, and, furthermore, the entirety of 1 Maccabees 9 is tied together by the figure of Bacchides.

As to the units in 1 Maccabees 10–11, let us observe the following. Martola has suggested that there is "a structural similarity" between the bulk of these chapters:

> We have before us a schematic course of events, a motif. A new pretender to the throne in Antioch having appeared and successfully claimed the throne, there is a description of Jonathan's winning the new king's favour despite resistance from enemies among his own people. From a structural point of view 10,1–66 and 10,67–11,37 are, consequently, parallels.[7]

According to Martola, we may outline this parallel as follows:

the success of the pretender to the throne	10:1–58	10:67–11:19
the success of Jonathan	10:59–66	11:20–37

I agree with Martola that 10:59–66 and 11:20–37 are similar, since they feature the episodes of Jonathan visiting royalty at Ptolemais, and I also agree that there is a structural similarity between 10:1–58 and 10:67–11:19. I believe, however, that Martola is mistaken about the nature of this latter similarity and therefore his labelling is flawed. For instance, the notion that 10:1–58 primarily presents the "success of the pretender to the throne" is off the mark, since the success of the pretender, Alexander Balas, in this material is largely limited to 10:46–58. In the earlier material it is Jonathan who meets with repeated success, not Alexander. This matter deserves close attention.

In 10:3–4 Demetrius I sends a letter to Jonathan to honor him and to make peace. 10:6 records that Demetrius gave Jonathan authority to recruit troops, to equip them, and to become his ally. He also ordered that some hostages in the citadel be released to Jonathan. After receiving this letter, Jonathan read it in the hearing of those in the citadel and they became "greatly alarmed when

[7] Martola, *Capture and Liberation,* 199.

they heard that the king had given him authority to recruit troops" (10:8), leading them to release the hostages to Jonathan.

Jonathan goes on, in 10:10, to take up residence in Jerusalem, and to rebuild and restore the city. At 10:11 he directs workers to build the walls and to encircle Mount Zion with fortifications, and they do so. According to 10:12–13, as a result of these fortifications "the foreigners who were in the strongholds that Bacchides had built fled; all of them left their places and went back to their own lands."

In 10:15–20 Alexander Balas hears of the promises made by Demetrius to Jonathan and writes his own letter to Jonathan. 10:20 is especially important, for, in this verse, Alexander appoints Jonathan to be high priest and to be a king's Friend. The verse also tells us that Alexander sent Jonathan a purple robe and a golden crown. 10:21 states: "So Jonathan put on the sacred vestments . . . and he recruited troops and equipped them with arms in abundance."

In 10:22–24 Demetrius is distressed that Alexander has "gotten ahead" of him in forming a friendship with the Jews, and so he decides to write yet another letter. This letter is lengthy, stretching from 10:25 to 10:45. Among other things, it promises additional tax exemptions, as well as the annexation of "the three districts . . . added to Judea from the country of Samaria" (10:38).[8]

Several commentators have called attention to the fact that Demetrius' letter at 10:25–45 is not addressed to Jonathan, but rather to the "nation of the Jews."[9] Some have speculated that the letter—if genuine—may have been intended to serve anti-Hasmonean aims by trying to win Jews away from Jonathan.[10] Such a view does not mean, however, that the letter is used in 1 Maccabees 10 with any anti-Hasmonean intent. On the contrary, it is likely that the author either misunderstood the text of the letter and used it unwittingly, or else knowingly adapted a hostile letter by shaping the way it would be understood in the context of the book.[11] As to the latter possibility, since it is placed after two other letters which are manifestly addressed to Jonathan

[8] Scholars generally hold that 10:38 refers to the three districts of Aphairema, Lydda, and Rathamin, which are named in 1 Macc 11:34.

[9] See especially Grimm, *Das erste Buch der Maccabäer,* 152.

[10] I will remind the reader that the authenticity of the letter is in dispute. See n. 25 in chapter two above.

[11] On the possibility of an unwitting use of 10:25–45, see Goldstein, *I Maccabees,* 405.

(see 10:3–4 and 10:18), the hearer/reader may naturally view 10:25–45 as simply one more in a series of letters in which it seems that two royal figures—Demetrius I and Alexander Balas—are trying to win Jonathan's support.[12]

In sum, we should consider 10:1–45 as representing Jonathan's success, and not, as Martola would have it, the success of Alexander.[13]

The situation is analogous with regard to 10:67–11:19, which Martola also designates as concerning "the success of the pretender to the throne." In this case Martola has Demetrius II in mind. The success of Demetrius II, however, is most evident in 11:9–19 and, once more, the majority of the material, supposedly about the success of the pretender, is, in actuality, about the success of Jonathan.

In 10:67 Demetrius II appears, and in 10:69 he appoints Apollonius to attack the Jews. Apollonius sends a message to threaten Jonathan that takes up 10:70–73. Jonathan sets out, with ten thousand men, to encounter Apollonius in 10:74–75. Jonathan gains possession of Joppa at 10:76 and, with it, some of Apollonius' troops. 10:77–85 records various conflicts between the Jewish forces and those of Apollonius. The final outcome is that the Jews, led by Jonathan, defeat Apollonius. Thus, at 10:86, when Jonathan encamps near Askalon, the people of the city come out to meet him with "great pomp." In the following verse, 10:87, Jonathan returns to Jerusalem "with a large amount of booty." In 10:88–89 Alexander Balas, after learning of Jonathan's victory over Apollonius, honors Jonathan further by sending him a golden buckle, "such as it is the custom to give to the King's Kinsmen."

Beginning with 11:1 Ptolemy VI enters the scene and attempts to gain control of Alexander's kingdom. Yet even in this material Jonathan is successful. When Ptolemy comes to Azotus, where Jonathan had chased some of Apollonius' men and had burned the temple of Dagon, some people show Ptolemy the corpses lying about and the charred bodies of those whom Jonathan had burned in order "to throw blame on" Jonathan. But 11:5 tells us that "the king kept silent," and in 11:6 Jonathan meets Ptolemy "at Joppa with pomp."

[12] Lending credence to this view is the wording of 10:46, immediately following the letter: "When *Jonathan* and the people heard these things. . . ."

[13] At 11:30–37 there is a letter from Demetrius II to Jonathan, which promises, among other things, some tax exemptions. As may be seen by his chart, Martola considers this letter to be part of "the success of Jonathan." If so, then why should the letters at 10:3–6, 15–20, 25–45 not represent Jonathan's success as well?

Thus, in both instances where Martola labels material as concerning "the success of the pretender to the throne" (10:1–58 and 10:67–11:19) it is actually Jonathan's success that is in the foreground, which is set against a backdrop of competition between Seleucid (and Ptolemaic) powers. With this situation in mind, I propose that we take a broader view of the material in order to observe Jonathan's success both before 10:1–66 and after 10:67–11:37.

On the one hand, before 10:1, we may begin at 9:1, since 8:1–32 concerns relations with Rome. After Judas dies while fighting against Bacchides, Jonathan accepts the leadership of the Hasmonean cause in 9:28–31. Eventually, he obtains peace from Bacchides, who swears never to bother Jonathan and the Jews again (9:70–72). 9:73 states that "the sword ceased from Israel" and relates that Jonathan "settled in Michmash and began to judge the people."

Regarding the material following 11:37, we may proceed up to the end of that chapter (11:74), since in 12:1 we again take up relations with Rome. In 11:41–42 Demetrius II agrees to remove troops from the citadel and other strongholds and tells Jonathan: "Not only will I do these things for you and your nation, but I will confer great honor on you and your nation, if I find an opportunity." Moving on, while Martola directs our attention to Alexander Balas and Demetrius II, we should not ignore the child king Antiochus VI, who claims the throne at 11:54. A letter is written in Antiochus' name to Jonathan at 11:57, in which he confirms Jonathan as high priest, allows Jonathan to annex some neighboring districts, and makes Jonathan one of the king's Friends. In addition, in 11:58, Antiochus sends Jonathan some gold plate and a table service, and grants him the right to drink from gold cups, to dress in purple, and to wear a gold buckle. In 11:60 all the army of Syria gather to Jonathan as allies, and he is again met by the inhabitants of Askalon, who pay him honor. Finally, in 11:63–74, Jonathan meets with success by defeating some officers of Demetrius II who had come to attack him.

To recap: in 9:1–10:66 we have a coherent story of the rise of Jonathan, from being a guerilla leader to becoming "a mighty one" in the Seleucid empire and a Friend of Alexander Balas,[14]and in 10:67–11:74 there is again

[14] It is interesting to observe that Doran (*The First Book of Maccabees,* 112) gives the heading "Jonathan's Rise to Power" to 9:23–73, and Goldstein (*I Maccabees,* 402) designates 10:22–66 as "Jonathan Grows in Power."

thematic coherence as Jonathan must struggle to maintain his status as a "mighty one" with new royal claimants—Demetrius II and Antiochus VI—when Alexander is killed (cf. 11:17).

Given the preceding observations, section two may be recast as follows.

A 8:1–32 Jewish mission to Rome
  B 9:1–10:66 Jonathan rises in power
  B′ 10:67–11:74 Jonathan maintains his powerful status
A′ 12:1–23 Jewish mission to Rome

This is obviously a tighter structure than that with which we began. The missions to Rome remain paired (AA′) and now Jonathan's visits to Ptolemais align as well (10:59–66 in B and 11:22–37 in B′). In addition, as we have seen, other parallels have come into focus regarding the successes of Jonathan vis-à-vis the Seleucid rulers. I may note, as an additional parallel between the proposed units 9:1–10:66 and 10:67–11:74, the fact that they conclude in a similar fashion:

10:66	11:74
καὶ ἐπέστρεψεν Ιωναθαν εἰς Ιερουσαλημ μετ' εἰρήνης καὶ εὐφροσύνης	καὶ ἐπέστρεψεν Ιωναθαν εἰς Ιερουσαλημ
And Jonathan returned to Jerusalem in peace and gladness.	And Jonathan returned to Jerusalem.

It will not have been lost on the reader that the structures I have identified for sections one (1:1–6:17) and two (8:1–12:23) to this point skip over the material from 6:18 to 7:50. It may be asked whether this material is somehow involved with section two. I suggested in chapter two that there is a similar pattern at work throughout 6:18–7:50; that is, three times a Jewish party complains to a king about Judas, and the king attempts to punish him. We must now investigate this matter more closely.

We will not begin with 1 Maccabees 6, however. Rather, let us first observe with Martola that there is a sequence of four Seleucid invasions into Judea in 1 Maccabees 7 and 9: (1) 7:5–25; (2) 7:26–50; (3) 9:1–57; and (4) 9:58–72. (The reader will recall that 8:1–32 interrupts this sequence.) It will be profitable for us to inquire who prompted each of these invasions.

The first invasion comes as a result of an accusation against Judas and his followers made to Demetrius I at 7:6–7 by "the lawless and godless men of Israel (ἄνδρες ἄνομοι καὶ ἀσεβεῖς ἐξ Ισραηλ); they were led by Alcimus, who wanted to be high priest" (7:5). Let us note that at 7:9 the text refers to "the godless Alcimus (Ἄλκιμον τὸν ἀσεβῆ)." The importance of this identification will be made clear below.

The second invasion comes after Alcimus again goes to Demetrius to complain about Judas and those with him. We are told in 7:25 that Alcimus "returned to the king and brought malicious charges against them."

The third invasion is, in Martola's words, the only one of the four "which does not begin expressly at the instigation of the evil ones in Israel."[15] Indeed, 9:1 states: "When Demetrius heard that Nicanor and his army had fallen in battle, he sent Bacchides and Alcimus into the land of Judah a second time. . . ."

The fourth invasion comes when "all the lawless (πάντες οἱ ἄνομοι)" plot to have Bacchides return, and go to him to consult with him (9:58–59).

As we have just seen, Martola implies that three of these invasions are due to "the instigation of the evil ones in Israel." While I agree in principle with this assertion, I believe it is crucial that we pay close attention to the terminology that is used. Thus, it is more accurate to state that the first invasion involves "lawless and godless" (ἄνομοι καὶ ἀσεβεῖς); the second, Alcimus the "godless" (ἀσεβῆ); and the fourth, "lawless" (ἄνομοι). It may be observed that the first two invasions have in common instigation by a "godless" party.

Bearing this latter point in mind—the use of the term ἀσεβής—let us look at another invasion, one that occurs shortly before 7:5–25. In 6:28–63 Antiochus V (with Lysias) leads an invasion of Judea. This invasion is instigated at 6:21–27. According to 6:19 Judas besieged the citadel, and then, in 6:21, "some of the garrison escaped the siege and some of the godless Israelites (τινες τῶν ἀσεβῶν ἐξ Ισραηλ) joined them" and they went to Antiochus and persuaded him to come to Judah (6:22–28). Thus, we encounter once more the use of the term ἀσεβής.[16]

The upshot of the preceding considerations is that it seems as though three invasions—6:28–63, 7:5–25, and 7:26–50—are linked together since

[15] Martola, *Capture and Liberation,* 168.

[16] Note the parallel between the ἀσεβῶν ἐξ Ισραηλ of 6:21 and the ἀσεβεῖς ἐξ Ισραηλ of 7:5.

each is instigated by a "godless" party and involves a king who attacks Judas and his followers. In contrast, the invasion at 9:1–57 is Demetrius' own idea, while the invasion at 9:58–72 is the result of the activity of "all the lawless," it involves a Friend of a king–Bacchides–and not the king himself, and, in any case, Judas is dead by that point, having been killed at 9:18. Thus, we may now confirm the notion that 6:18–7:50 presents a thematically coherent unit: three times, a "godless" entity persuades a king to punish Judas, a pattern that is broken, in different ways, by 8:1–32, 9:1–57, and 9:58–72. If we regard 6:18–7:50 as a single unit, we have the following structure for section two.

A 6:18–7:50 three invasions prompted by "godless" parties
  B 8:1–32 Jewish mission to Rome
    C 9:1–10:66 Jonathan rises in power
    C′ 10:67–11:74 Jonathan maintains his powerful status
  B′ 12:1–23 Jewish mission to Rome
A′ ?

It remains to determine the limits of A′. In my view, a reasonable suggestion is 12:24–14:15. Simon becomes the leader in this material, which culminates in a poem that glorifies his achievements (14:4–15). Thus, there is thematic coherence to such a unit. I also observed in chapter two that 14:16 seems to offer a new beginning. In addition, the poem at 14:4–15 appears to make contact with a number of statements and motifs from earlier parts of the book, almost as if summarizing much of what has gone before. Let us observe the following items.

(1) The first sentence of the poem is: "The land had rest (καὶ ἡσύχασεν ἡ γῆ) all the days of Simon." There are two other occasions in the book when the similar phrase καὶ ἡσύχασεν ἡ γῆ Ιουδα ("the land of Judah had rest") appears. In 7:50 we read: "So the land of Judah had rest (καὶ ἡσύχασεν ἡ γῆ 'Ιούδα) for a few days." 9:57 states: "When Bacchides saw that Alcimus was dead, he returned to the king, and the land of Judah had rest (καὶ ἡσύχασεν ἡ γῆ Ιουδα) for two years." The use of these phrases is fascinating in that they appear once each in association with the three brothers–Judas, Jonathan, and Simon. At 7:50 Judas has led the Jews to victory over Nicanor. At 9:57 Jonathan is the leader of the Hasmonean cause. 14:4 is obviously used in reference to Simon.

(2) Still in 14:4, we have the phrase "all the/his days (πάσας τὰς ἡμέρας)," which appears twice in the verse. First, as we have just seen, we are told that "the land had rest all the days of Simon." Second, we read that Simon's rule

was pleasing to the Jews, "as was the honor shown him, all his days." The phrase πάσας τὰς ἡμέρας appears a total of four other times in 1 Maccabees (2:65; 3:12; 9:71; 10:47). The most interesting, from the viewpoint of 14:4, is the first appearance, in 2:65. In this verse Mattathias says the following to his sons: "Here is your brother Simeon who, I know, is wise in counsel; always listen to him (ἀκούετε πάσας τὰς ἡμέρας); he shall be your father." It is tempting to see in 14:4 a nod back to 2:65.

(3) 14:9 relates that, in Simon's time, "old men (πρεσβύτεροι) sat in the streets; they all talked together of good things, and the youths (νεανίσκοι) put on splendid military attire." The only other verse in 1 Maccabees which mentions both "old men" and "youths" is 1:26, part of a lament following the plundering of the Jerusalem temple by Antiochus IV: "[Israel mourned deeply in every community,] rulers and elders (πρεσβύτεροι) groaned, young women and young men (νεανίσκοι) became faint, the beauty of the women faded." Thus, the situation described in 1:26 is reversed in 14:9.

(4) In 14:10 we are told, concerning Simon, that "his renown spread to the ends of the earth (ὠνομάσθη τὸ ὄνομα τῆς δόξης αὐτοῦ ἕως ἄκρου γῆς)." This assertion resonates with the declaration at 3:9, in a poem concerning Judas, that "he was renowned to the ends of the earth (καὶ ὠνομάσθη ἕως ἐσχάτου γῆς)."

(5) In 14:11 the text relates that Simon established peace in the land, and thus "Israel rejoiced with great joy (εὐφροσύνην μεγάλην)." We find the expression "great joy" at three earlier points in the book:

> There was very great joy (μεγάλη εὐφροσύνη) among the people. (4:58)
>
> And [Judas] led them to Judea with great rejoicing (εὐφροσύνης μεγάλης). (5:23)
>
> The people rejoiced greatly and celebrated that day as a day of great gladness (εὐφροσύνης μεγάλην). (7:48)

The first case (4:58) is in reference to the restoration of the temple. The second occasion (5:23) is when Judas has rescued some Jews from the local Gentiles who had threatened them, and takes them to Jerusalem. The third instance (7:48) refers to the defeat of Nicanor and the inauguration of the festival which celebrated his demise, Nicanor Day.[17]

[17] For discussions of this festival, see Grimm, *Das erste Buch der Maccabäer,* 118, and Abel, *Les Livres des Maccabées,* 144.

(6) 14:13–14, near the ending of the poem, seems to reflect the opening units of the book.

> No one was left in the land to fight them, and the kings were crushed in those days. [Simon] gave help to all the humble among his people; he sought out the law, and did away with all the lawless (πάντα ἄνομον) and outlaws. (14:13–14)

The reader will recall that the first two units of 1 Maccabees introduce us to the enemies of the faithful Jews. There are two troublesome groups. First, in 1:1–10 we meet various kings–Alexander the Great and his "sons," including Antiochus IV. It is, of course, primarily the Seleucid royal claimants with whom the Jews grapple in 1 Maccabees. Second, in 1:11–15 lawless Jews (υἱοὶ παράνομοι) emerge and make a covenant with the Gentiles. These lawless Jews obviously cause a great deal of trouble for the faithful Jews in 1 Maccabees. Thus, the kings and the lawless who are mentioned in 14:13–14 echo the topics of 1:1–10 and 1:11–15.[18]

(7) The poem ends, in 14:15, with the statement that "the sanctuary [Simon] made glorious, and he added to the vessels of the sanctuary (τὰ σκεύη τῶν ἁγίων)."[19] This wording is similar to that found in 4:49, in reference to the temple restoration: "They made new holy vessels (σκεύη ἅγια καινὰ)."

Taking all of this evidence into account, the poem at 14:4–15 does seem to provide a good ending point for section two. If we consider 12:24–14:15 to

[18] Indeed, in several places the poem for Simon (14:4–15) reflects the opening verses of the book. Consider the following. First, 1:2 tells us that Alexander the Great "put to death the kings of the earth," while, as we have just seen, 14:13 asserts that in Simon's day "the kings were crushed." Second, I noted above the similarity of the statement in 14:4 that "the land had rest (καὶ ἡσύχασεν ἡ γῆ) all the days of Simon" to those occasions in the book when the phrase καὶ ἡσύχασεν ἡ γῆ Ιουδα ("the land of Judah had rest") appears. We may note, though, that the wording in 14:4 also resonates with that of 1:3, which states that "when the earth became quiet before him [sc. Alexander the Great] (καὶ ἡσύχασεν ἡ γῆ ἐνώπιον αὐτου) . . . his heart was lifted up." Third, 1:4 informs us that Alexander the Great ruled over both "countries" (χωρῶν) and "nations" (ἐθνῶν), while 14:6 records that Simon "extended the borders of his nation (ἔθνει)" and "gained full control of the country (χώρας)."

[19] It is interesting to note that this statement is chiastic:

A τὰ ἅγια
  B ἐδόξασε
  B′ καὶ ἐπλήθυνε
A′ τὰ σκεύη τῶν ἁγίων

be a single unit, we have, as a final result, the following as the proposed structure of section two.

A 6:18–7:50 ?
  B 8:1–32 Jewish mission to Rome
    C 9:1–10:66 Jonathan rises in power
    C 10:67–11:74 Jonathan maintains his powerful status
  B′ 12:1–23 Jewish mission to Rome
A′ 12:24–14:15 ?

I have left A and A′ without topic headings, and placed question marks in their stead, since it is not the case that A′ mirrors the pattern of "godless" entities instigating invasions that we observed in A.[20] Still, an indication that we appear to be on the right track overall is the fact that this chiastic arrangement brings a seeming frame into view. First, let us consider some similar material in 6:19 and 12:35.

> Judas therefore resolved to destroy them [sc. the garrison in the citadel], and assembled all the people (καὶ ἐξεκκλησίασε πάντα τὸν λαὸν) to besiege them. (6:19)

> When Jonathan returned he convened the elders of the people (καὶ ἐξεκκλησίασε τοὺς πρεσβυτέρους τοῦ λαοῦ) and planned with them to build strongholds in Judea, [to build the walls of Jerusalem still higher, and to erect a barrier between the citadel and the city]. (12:35)

The repetition of the verb ἐξεκλησιάζω is striking since the word is a rarity both in 1 Maccabees, where it appears only these two times, and in the LXX as a whole (eleven total appearances).[21] To be sure, different characters are involved in these verses, but there is a similarity of intention to assemble the people. In each case the people are brought together—at least in part—to attack the citadel in some way (to besiege it in 6:19, and to erect a barrier between the citadel and the city in 12:35–36). It may be observed that these verses appear near the beginnings of the units AA′ above.

As to the rest of the frame, the endings of AA′ are similar. To be specific, the last three verses of A (7:48–50) are mirrored in the closing material of A′.

[20] The word ἀσεβής does not even appear in A′ (12:24–14:15).

[21] In addition to 1 Macc 6:19 and 12:35, ἐξεκλησιάζω appears in Lev 8:4; Num 20:10; Judg 20:1; 2 Sam 20:14; 1 Kgs 12:21; Jer 33:9; 1 Chr 13:5, 15:3, 28:1.

(1) In 7:48 we are told that the Jews rejoice because of their triumph over Nicanor and celebrate with "great joy" (εὐφροσύνης μεγάλην). As we have seen, this expression also appears at 14:11.

(2) In 7:49 it is decreed that the defeat of Nicanor should be an annual celebration. In 13:51 the Jews enter the citadel and, in 13:52, Simon decrees that this event should be commemorated annually as well. Compare the similarity of the following material.

7:49	13:52
καὶ ἔστησαν	καὶ ἔστησε
τοῦ ἄγειν	κατ᾽ ἐνιαυτὸν
κατ᾽ ἐνιαυτὸν	τοῦ ἄγειν
τὴν ἡμέραν ταύτην	τὴν ἡμέραν ταύτην
They decreed	Simon decreed
that this day	that every year
should be celebrated	they should celebrate
each year	this day

(3) In 7:50 we are told that "the land of Judah had rest (καὶ ἡσύχασεν ἡ γῆ Ἰούδα)" for a few days. As we have seen, a similar expression also appears at 14:4.

Thus, the beginnings of AA′ feature similar phrases concerning gathering people to attack the citadel, while the endings contain additional instances of similar wording. Section two appears to be framed by these correspondences.

In sum, it seems reasonable to propose that section two (6:18–14:15) has a chiastic structure, though the thematic relationship between A (6:18–7:50) and A′ (12:24–14:15), if any, is not readily apparent. As with the possible chiastic structure of section one, I will seek further evidence in the next chapter that will allow us to accept or to reject the proposed chiasm.

Section Three

The reader may wonder about the material following 14:15, with which we ended section two. Since this material does not involve any rare words identified as promising indicators of structure in the preceding chapter, I have no reason to arrange 14:16–16:24 (section three) in any particular structural pattern. I will note, however, that 14:17 and 16:24 present an inclusio.

> When [the Romans] heard that [Jonathan's] brother Simon had become high priest (γέγονεν ἀρχιερεὺς) in his stead, and that he was ruling over the country and the towns in it, [they wrote to him]. (14:17)
>
> [The rest of the acts of John Hyrcanus] are written in the annals of his high priesthood, after the time that he became high priest (ἐγενήθη ἀρχιερεὺς) after his father. (16:24)

In each case someone has become high priest–Simon or his son, John. These are the only two uses of the collocation γίνομαι plus ἀρχιερεύς in 1 Maccabees. This situation suggests that we should consider section three as a single literary unit.[22]

Conclusion

I will discuss section three in detail in chapter seven below. In the following two chapters, however, I will investigate further the chiastic structures that I have proposed for sections one and two. In chapter five I will take up similarities between paired units in the chiastic structures. In chapter six I will explore various thematic issues.

[22] I might add that this consideration strengthens the notion that 14:15 is an ending.

CHAPTER 5

Formal Symmetries within Sections One and Two (1:1–14:15)

In this chapter I will explore the paired units of sections one and two in order to determine if there is evidence to support the proposed architecture of these sections that was presented in the previous chapter. To facilitate my discussion I will henceforth refer to the paired units (subsections) of section one as 1.AA′, 1.BB′, and so forth. Similarly, I will refer to the paired units (subsections) of section two as 2.AA′, 2.BB′, and so on.

1.AA′

1.A (1:1–10) briefly reviews the career of Alexander the Great, as well as his death. After he dies, his successors emerge, and among their descendants is Antiochus IV. 1.A′ (6:1–17) centers on the death of Antiochus IV. Thus, Antiochus IV is introduced in 1.A and dies in 1.A′.

It is interesting that 1.A′ begins with an episode in which Antiochus desires to plunder a temple in Elymais. There is no further mention of Elymais in 1 Maccabees, and, immediately after failing to plunder the temple, Antiochus sets out to leave the area. Martola observes:

> It appears . . . that the author is hardly at all interested in the campaign in the eastern half of the Empire. Only the first four verses [6:1–4] are devoted to the campaign, and they limit themselves to telling about the unsuccessful attempt to capture the city of Elymais. The main part of the passage

[6:5–16] in reality deals with the effect upon the king's life of earlier courses of events in Palestine.[1]

While we can well understand that a depiction of the death of Antiochus IV is important in 1 Maccabees, we must ask why 1.A′ prefaces his death with the material about Elymais. According to the text, he does not die there (cf. 6:4). Further, the account of the attempt to plunder the temple is not necessary in order to set the stage for Antiochus' death. What leads to his death is hearing about the Jews' victories over Lysias and the liberation of the temple (cf. 6:5–9).[2]

In this light, the way that the riches of Elymais are described is intriguing:

> King Antiochus . . . heard that Elymais in Persia was a city famed for its wealth in silver and gold. Its temple was very rich, containing golden shields, breastplates, and weapons *left there by Alexander. . . .*" (6:1–2)

It is tempting to conclude that the material about Elymais is provided because it allows Alexander the Great to be mentioned again, thus creating a bridge to connect 1.A with 1.A′.[3]

[1] Martola, *Capture and Liberation*, 194. Though 1 Macc 6:1 refers to Elymais as a city (πόλις), it was actually a region (the biblical Elam). See Grimm, *Das erste Buch der Maccabäer*, 91, and Abel, *Les Livres des Maccabées*, 108.

[2] Indeed, if the material concerning Elymais (6:1b–4) had been omitted it would not be missed: "King Antiochus was going through the upper provinces when . . . someone came to him in Persia and reported that the armies that had gone into the land of Judah had been routed" (6:1a, 5).

[3] 1 Maccabees is one of the two oldest extant sources on the death of Antiochus IV, the other being Polybius. (For a study of the sources, see the appendix, "Antiochus IV and the Temple of Nanaia," in W. W. Tarn, *The Greeks in Bactria and India* [3d ed.; Chicago: Ares, 1984] 463–66.) At xxxi 9, Polybius (*The Histories* [LCL; New York: Putnam's, 1927] 6. 177) states:

> In Syria King Antiochus, wishing to provide himself with money, decided to make an expedition against the sanctuary of Artemis in Elymais. On reaching the spot he was foiled in his hopes, as the barbarian tribes who dwelt in the neighbourhood would not permit the outrage, and on his retreat he died at Tabae in Persia, smitten with madness, as some people say, owing to certain manifestations of divine displeasure when he was attempting this outrage on the above sanctuary.

We should also consider the account of Appian, *Syrian Wars* xi 66 (*Appian's Roman History* [LCL; Cambridge, MA: Harvard University, 1962] 2. 233), who writes: "[Antiochus] was terrified and withdrew from [Egypt], and robbed the temple of Venus of Elymais; he then died of a wasting disease."

As may be seen, there is no mention of Alexander the Great in either of these pagan passages

In this regard, we should recall that Alexander the Great is mentioned in 1 Maccabees only in 1.AA′. He is referred to by name at the outset of each subsection, in similar ways.

> καὶ ἐγένετο μετὰ τὸ πατάξαι Ἀλέξανδρον τὸν Φιλίππου τὸν Μακεδόνα, ὃς ἐξῆλθεν ἐκ τῆς γῆς Χεττιιμ καὶ ἐπάταξε τὸν Δαρεῖον βασιλέα Περσῶν καὶ Μήδων καὶ ἐβασίλευσεν ἀντ' αὐτοῦ πρότερον ἐπὶ τὴν Ἑλλάδα (1:1)
>
> After Alexander son of Philip, the Macedonian, who came from the land of Kittim, had defeated King Darius of the Persians and the Medes, he succeeded him as king. (He had previously become king of Greece.)
>
> καὶ τὸ ἱερὸν τὸ ἐν αὐτῇ πλούσιον σφόδρα, καὶ ἐκεῖ καλύμματα χρυσᾶ καὶ θώρακες καὶ ὅπλα, ἃ κατέλιπεν ἐκεῖ Ἀλέξανδρος ὁ τοῦ Φιλίππου ὁ βασιλεὺς ὁ Μακεδών, ὃς ἐβασίλευσε πρῶτος ἐν τοῖς Ἕλλησι (6:2)
>
> Its temple was very rich, containing golden shields, breastplates, and weapons left there by Alexander son of Philip, the Macedonian king who first reigned over the Greeks.

The repeated identification "Macedonian" is striking, since this terminology reveals an awareness of the difference between Macedonians and Greeks. In addition, the concluding comments—"he had previously become king of Greece" (1:1) and the "king who first reigned over the Greeks" (6:2)—were presumably closer in the original Hebrew.[4]

(*pace* Goldstein [*I Maccabees*, 308], who comments that "our author's account is in harmony with that of the reliable pagan historians Polybius (xxxi 9) and Appian (xi 66)"). Thus, Alexander was not a necessary component of the tale. It would seem, then, that the author of 1 Macc 6:1–17 either happened to find Alexander mentioned in some other source about Antiochus' attempt to plunder a temple and thought it attractive to use for structural symmetry, or, more likely given the evidence of Polybius and Appian, introduced Alexander into the account for the same purpose.

[4] Cf. Dancy (*A Commentary on I Maccabees*, 55), who comments as follows on 1:1.

> Gk. πρότερον ἐπὶ τὴν Ἑλλάδα. It should be obvious . . . that the Greek will not do. Fortunately it is equally obvious from 6.2 what the author meant: Alexander was the first of the Greek . . . emperors. . . . For ἐπὶ τὴν Ἑλλάδα we must have, as in 6.2, ἐν τοῖς Ἕλλησιν, because the abstract noun is not used in the wider sense; that is only a matter of a slight mistranslation of the Hebrew. For πρότερον we require πρῶτος as in 6.2 . . . but again the trouble is due to a mistranslation of the Hebrew, in which language there are no comparatives and superlatives.

Notice how Dancy takes for granted that 6:2 parallels 1:1.

Beyond the correspondences concerning the descriptions of Alexander the Great, we have already observed in chapter one above that there are impressive similarities between his death in 1.A and the death of Antiochus IV in 1.A′. It is interesting that the dying process for Antiochus is longer than the corresponding process for Alexander. Whereas Alexander's death process takes place over three verses (1:5–7), Antiochus' is strung out over nine verses (6:8–16). As I mentioned in chapter two, we read several times in 6:1–17 of the grief suffered by Antiochus IV, which gives the impression of providing a cathartic release. By lengthening his death process, the narrative contributes further to this catharsis.[5] 1.A′ thus closes out section one on a satisfying note for the ancient Jewish hearer/reader.[6]

In sum, the resemblances between the episodes of dying kings, together with the additional material concerning Alexander the Great, serve to link 1.A and 1.A′, and, in the process, to frame section one.[7]

[5] On the use of delay for the sake of emphasis, see Bar-Efrat, *Narrative Art*, 161.

[6] Other factors in 6:1–17 add to the cathartic release for the ancient Jewish hearer/reader, including the fact that Antiochus recognizes his maltreatment of the Jews, as well as how he dies in a strange land, away from a proper resting place with his ancestors (cf. 6:12–13). See Doran, *The First Book of Maccabees*, 85.

[7] There is a discrepancy between the accounts of Antiochus' death in 1 and 2 Maccabees. In 1 Maccabees, as we have seen, Antiochus dies after the liberation of the temple. In 2 Maccabees, however, he dies before the temple is cleansed (cf. 2 Maccabees 9–10). With the mid-century discovery of a list of Seleucid kings (see A. J Sachs and D. J. Wiseman, "A Babylonian King List of the Hellenistic Period," *Iraq* 16 [1954] 202–11), the sequence given by 2 Maccabees has come to be preferred by scholars. For instance, Collins (*Daniel, First Maccabees, Second Maccabees*, 190–91) comments:

> It now appears that [Antiochus] died in November or December of 164 BCE very shortly before the consecration [of the temple]. The news probably did not reach Jerusalem until afterwards. 1 Maccabees, however, wishes to dramatize the death of the great tyrant. His decline is attributed to frustration and disappointment, but especially to grief over what had happened in Jerusalem. He even feels remorse over his treatment of the Jews. This kind of moralizing fiction is common in ancient historiography. . . .

Given the material I have presented in the text above, it may also be that the placement of the death of Antiochus in 1 Maccabees after the liberation of the temple was at least partially due to structural considerations. Indeed, it is not hard to see that by having Antiochus die after the consecration of the temple the narrative gains structural balance between 1.A and 1.A′, and also makes a strong moralistic point.

1.BB′

We are told in 1.B (1:11–15) about certain "renegades" among the Jews who wish to join with their Gentile neighbors. Some of these Jews gain permission to observe various Gentile practices and thus they abandon covenant loyalty. 1.B′ (5:1–68) serves as a contrasting narrative. In this material local Gentiles threaten to destroy the Jews in their midst, but Judas and his brothers–righteous Jews–come to their aid.

The contrast between the two subsections is clearly drawn in their opening verses, which were provided in the previous chapter. The reader will recall that in 1:11 (1.B) the renegade Jews want to make a covenant with the Gentiles around them (τῶν ἐθνῶν τῶν κύκλῳ ἡμῶν), but in 5:1–2 (1.B′) the Gentiles all around (τὰ ἔθνη κυκλόθεν) want to destroy the Jews.

The opening of 1.B′, then, clearly implies the danger and foolishness of the desire expressed by the renegades in 1.B to join with the Gentiles around them. The body of 1.B′ makes it plain what these Gentiles are like: again and again, we are told that they want to annihilate the Jews (cf. 5:9–10, 14–15, 27). Of course, throughout 1.B′ Judas, his brothers, and their forces are able to turn back the danger posed by the local Gentiles, and repeatedly the Gentiles are defeated. Thus, the victories of the faithful Jews of 1.B′ offset the dangerous desires of the renegade Jews of 1.B. It is interesting to note, in this regard, that 1.B′ (68 verses) is much longer than 1.B (5 verses). As a result, in 1.B′ the Jewish hearer/reader is provided another opportunity for cathartic release through the many instances of Jewish victories over Gentiles.

Both 1.B and 1.B′ contain several references to Gentiles. Of the combined fifteen uses of ἔθνος in 1.BB′, most stand alone (that is, they are simple references to "the Gentiles"),[8] but in five cases we have the expression "the Gentiles around," which appears in four instances (1:11; 5:10, 38, 57) as "the Gentiles around us."[9] While the word ἔθνος is not rare in the LXX, the phrase "the Gentiles around us" is. The word ἔθνος is found together with the word κύκλος ("around") but fifteen times in the LXX and in only six instances does the phrase "the Gentiles around us" appear: two times in Nehemiah (5:17; 6:16) and four times in 1 Maccabees, all of which are in 1.BB′.

[8] 1:13, 14, 15; 5:9, 19, 21 (bis), 22, 43, 63.

[9] The additional usage of the expression "the Gentiles around" occurs in 5:1.

Thus, thematic symmetries, supported by instances of specific wording, link 1.B and 1.B′.[10]

1.CC′

In 1.C (1:16–64) the temple is plundered by Antiochus IV, the citadel is constructed, and the Jewish cult is prohibited. At 1:59 the Greeks offer a pagan sacrifice in the temple. In 1.C′ (4:36–61) the Jewish rebels liberate the temple, and it is restored and purified. A strong connection between these two subsections is signaled by the opening words of 1.C′ (4:36), wherein the Jews set out to reverse the desecrated status of the temple and its altar that had been brought about by the Greeks in 1.C.

There are several thematic and verbal symmetries between these two subsections. First, many of the ritual objects stolen by Antiochus in 1:21–23 are specifically mentioned as having been restored by the Jews in 4:47–57. In 1:21–23 Antiochus takes the following: the golden altar (τὸ θυσιαστήριον τὸ χρυσοῦν); the lampstand for the light (τὴν λυχνίαν τοῦ φωτὸς) and all its utensils (πάντα τὰ σκεύη αὐτῆς); the table for the bread of the Presence (τὴν τράπεζαν τῆς προθέσεως); cups (τὰ σπονδεῖα); bowls (τὰς φιάλας); golden censers (τὰς θυίσκας τὰς χρυσᾶς); the curtain (τὸ καταπέτασμα); crowns (τοὺς στεφάνους); the gold decoration on the front of the temple (τὸν κόσμον τὸν χρυσοῦν τὸν κατὰ πρόσωπον τοῦ ναοῦ); silver and gold (τὸ ἀργύριον καὶ τὸ χρυσίον); costly vessels (τὰ σκεύη τὰ ἐπιθυμητὰ); and also "the hidden treasures (τοὺς θησαυροὺς τοὺς ἀποκρύφους)." Of these items, six are referred to in 1.C′ as well: the altar; the lampstand; the table; the curtain; the crowns; and the golden decoration on the front of the temple. The following material contains the pertinent references to the first four of these items that are referred to in 1.C′.

[10] Though the wars with local Gentiles are narrated all together in 1 Maccabees 5, they appear over several chapters in 2 Maccabees. (Sievers [*The Hasmoneans*, 49–51] provides a helpful synopsis of the pertinent material in the two books.) Further, as 1 Maccabees has it, the wars take place between the rededication of the temple (in 1.C′) and the death of Antiochus (in 1.A′). Scholars have often noted the difficulty of fitting the conflicts into this interval, and have thus held that 1 Maccabees has squeezed into a continuous presentation events that actually took place over a longer period of time. (See, e.g., Dancy, *A Commentary on I Maccabees*, 21–22.) Once again, it may be that the author deals with the material in this manner for structural reasons, both by assembling all of the material in one place (1.B′), and by arranging the local wars to follow the liberation of the temple and to precede Antiochus' death. In both respects, the material then offsets 1.B.

> καὶ ἔλαβον λίθους ὁλοκλήρους κατὰ τὸν νόμον καὶ ᾠκοδόμησαν θυσιαστήριον καινὸν κατὰ τὸ πρότερον καὶ ᾠκοδόμησαν τὰ ἅγια καὶ τὰ ἐντὸς τοῦ οἴκου καὶ τὰς αὐλὰς ἡγίασαν καὶ ἐποίησαν σκεύη ἅγια καινὰ καὶ εἰσήνεγκαν τὴν λυχνίαν καὶ τὸ θυσιαστήριον τῶν θυμιαμάτων καὶ τὴν τράπεζαν εἰς τὸν ναόν καὶ ἐθυμίασαν ἐπὶ τὸ θυσιαστήριον καὶ ἐξῆψαν τοὺς λύχνους τοὺς ἐπὶ τῆς λυχνίας, καὶ ἐφαίνοσαν ἐν τῷ ναῷ καὶ ἐπέθηκαν ἐπὶ τὴν τράπεζαν ἄρτους καὶ ἐξεπέτασαν τὰ καταπετάσματα καὶ ἐτέλεσαν πάντα τὰ ἔργα, ἃ ἐποίησαν (4:47–51)

> Then they [sc. "priests devoted to the law"] took unhewn stones, as the law directs, and built a new altar like the former one. They also rebuilt the sanctuary and the interior of the temple, and consecrated the courts. They made new holy vessels, and brought the lampstand, the altar of incense, and the table into the temple. Then they offered incense on the altar and lit the lamps on the lampstand, and these gave light in the temple. They placed the bread on the table and hung up the curtains. Thus they finished all the work they had undertaken.

It may be seen that this material also contains a reference to "new holy vessels (σκεύη ἅγια καινὰ)," which, while not specifically relating to either the vessels accompanying the lampstand or the "costly vessels" that were stolen in 1.C, nevertheless does repeat the word σκεῦος. The fifth and sixth repeated items (the crowns and the gold decoration on the front of the temple) are restored in 4:57—"They decorated the front of the temple with golden crowns and small shields (στεφάνοις χρυσοῖς καὶ ἀσπιδίσκαις)." Of the repeated items, three only appear in 1 Maccabees in 1.CC′: (1) λυχνία in 1:21 and 4:49, 50; (2) τράπεζα in 1:22 and 4:49, 50; and (3) καταπέτασμα in 1:22 and 4:51.

A second connection between 1.C and 1.C′ comes through the desecration of the altar by the Greeks and the subsequent dedication of a new altar by the Jews.

> On the twenty-fifth day of the month (καὶ πέμπτῃ καὶ εἰκάδι τοῦ μηνὸς) [sc. Chislev; cf. 1:54] they [sc. the Greeks] offered sacrifice on the altar that was on top of the altar of burnt offering. (1:59)

> Early in the morning on the twenty-fifth day of the ninth month (τῇ πέμπτῃ καὶ εἰκάδι τοῦ μηνὸς τοῦ ἐνάτου), which is the month of Chislev, in the one hundred forty-eighth year, [the Jews] rose and offered sacrifice, as the law directs, on the new altar of burnt offering that they had built. (4:52–53)

As we have seen previously, the strong connectedness between these events is made manifest by 4:54 ("At the very season and on the very day that the Gentiles had profaned it [the altar] was dedicated"). It is important to notice that 4:54 is superfluous. The combination of 1:54 (wherein the month of Chislev is named) and 1:59 make clear the date on which the sacrifice of 1:59 took place, and it is plain that the action of 4:52–53 is on the same date. Thus, there is no chance for confusion concerning the fact that the dedication of the new altar occurred on the same date as the pagan sacrifice. In this light, we may see that 4:54 underscores the connection between 1.C and 1.C′ through repetition.[11]

A third connection between 1.C and 1.C′ concerns some fortifications. 1.C′ ends with a tag (4:60–61) which describes the fortification of Mount Zion by Jews. This report is very similar to a passage in 1.C (1:33–34) in which Greeks fortify the City of David.[12] The following is provided for the sake of comparison.

1:33–34	4:60–61
καὶ ᾠκοδόμησαν	καὶ ᾠκοδόμησαν
	ἐν τῷ καιρῷ ἐκείνῳ
τὴν πόλιν Δαυιδ	τὸ ὄρος Σιων κυκλόθεν
τείχει μεγάλῳ	τείχη ὑψηλὰ
καὶ ὀχυρῷ, πύργοις ὀχυροῖς	καὶ πύργους ὀχυρούς,
καὶ ἐγένετο αὐτοῖς εἰς ἄκραν	
	μήποτε παραγενηθέντα τὰ ἔθνη
	καταπατήσωσιν αὐτά, ὡς
	ἐποίησαν τὸ πρότερον
καὶ ἔθηκαν ἐκεῖ	καὶ ἀπέταξεν ἐκεῖ
ἔθνος ἁμαρτωλόν,	δύναμιν τηρεῖν αὐτὸ
ἄνδρας παρανόμους	

[11] Note that 4:59 further emphasizes the date of the twenty-fifth of Chislev: "Then Judas and his brothers and all the assembly of Israel determined that every year at that season the days of dedication of the altar should be observed with joy and gladness for eight days, beginning with the twenty-fifth day of the month of Chislev."

[12] This similarity was seen by Abel (*Les Livres des Maccabeés*, 87), who wrote: "Les termes employés [in 4:60] pour dépeindre les travaux de fortification de l'esplanade du Temple sont ceux qu'on a déjà vus 1,33 à propos de l'Acra."

Then [the Greeks] fortified	[The Jews] fortified
	at that time
the city of David	Mount Zion
with a great strong wall	with high walls
and strong towers,	and strong towers all around,
and it became their citadel.	
	to keep the Gentiles from
	coming and trampling them
	down as they had done before.
They stationed there a sinful	Judas stationed a garrison
people, men who were renegades.	there to guard it.

The correspondence between these verses is important, for while the material in 1.C′ concerning the restoration of the temple and the dedication of a new altar may perhaps be at least partly explained as being inherent repetition, the similarity of the material relating to the fortifications seems contrived.

A fourth connection between 1.C and 1.C′ may be found in the following contrast.

1:64	4:58
καὶ ἐγένετο	καὶ ἐγενήθη
ὀργὴ μεγάλη	μεγάλη εὐφροσύνη
ἐπὶ Ισραηλ σφόδρα	ἐν τῷ λαῷ σφόδρα
Very great wrath	There was very great joy
came upon Israel	among the people

Each of these sentences occurs either at the end or near the end of one of the subsections.[13] To be specific, 1:64 closes 1.C, and 4:58 is but three verses from the end of 1.C′ (4:61), appearing immediately before the tag concerning the fortification of Mount Zion.

It is obvious, then, that 1.C′ offsets 1.C in some major ways. The temple is robbed in 1.C, but many of the stolen items are restored in 1.C′. The altar is desecrated by a pagan sacrifice in 1.C, but a new altar is dedicated (on the same date) in 1.C′. In 1.C Greeks fortify the City of David, but in 1.C′ Jews

[13] We may observe another chiastic inclusio in the combination ὀργὴ μεγάλη (1:64)/ μεγάλη εὐφροσύνη (4:58). On the use of this device in biblical literature, see G. E. Howard, "Stylistic Inversion and the Synoptic Tradition," *JBL* 97 (1978) 375–89.

fortify Mount Zion. The culmination of the events of 1.C is that great wrath has come upon Israel, but the culmination of the events of 1.C′ is that there is now great joy among the people.

1.DD′

In 1.D (2:1–70) we are told the story of Mattathias: his rebellion against Antiochus IV, his final words to his sons, and his death. In 1.D′ (3:27–4:35) Antiochus IV becomes angered by the Jewish defiance of him, and he sends Lysias to quash the Jewish revolt.

The opening words of 1.D′ appear to be linked to 1.D. In 3:27 we are told that Antiochus, once he learned about the Jewish successes, became enraged: "When Antiochus heard these reports, he had wrathful anger (ὠργίσθη θυμῷ)." This wording resonates with a statement made by Mattathias at the outset of his testament in 1.D: "It is a time of ruin and wrathful anger (ὀργὴ θυμοῦ)" (2:49). The collocation of ὀργή/ὀργίζω with θυμός is striking, since it only occurs in 1 Maccabees three times: these two instances, plus 9:69. There are, then, two uses of the collocation in section one, and one use in section two. Of the two uses in section one, both occur in 1.DD′: in 1.D Mattathias warns that it is a time of "wrathful anger," and at the outset of 1.D′ Antiochus indeed has "wrathful anger."

The notion that there is a connection between 1.D and 1.D′ here is strengthened by the following. In 2:62–63 Mattathias tells his sons: "Of the words of a sinful man (ἀνδρὸς ἁμαρτωλοῦ) be not afraid, because his glory shall become dung and worms. Today he may be exalted, but tomorrow he will nowhere be found, because he has returned to his dust, and memory of him will have perished." It is a common view among commentators that this statement alludes to Antiochus IV, who is called a "sinful root (ῥίζα ἁμαρτωλὸς)" in 1:10.[14] Thus, in 1.D Mattathias says not to fear the words of a sinful man (= Antiochus IV), and in 1.D′ we read about Antiochus instructing Lysias to annihilate the Jews (cf. 3:35).[15]

[14] See, e.g., Grimm, *Das erste Buch der Maccabäer*, 49; Abel, *Les Livres des Maccabées*, 49; Nelis, *1 Makkabeeën*, 89; and Goldstein, *I Maccabees*, 241–42. In the light of 2:62–63, 2:48 possibly refers to Antiochus as well. This verse reads: "They rescued the law out of the hands of the Gentiles and kings, and they never let the sinner (τῷ ἁμαρτωλῷ) gain the upper hand."

[15] I might add that, assuming 2:62–63 does refer to Antiochus and his order of annihilation, it is striking for Antiochus to command Lysias at 3:35 "to banish the memory of [the Jews]," since Mattathias states that the "memory of him [= Antiochus]" will perish instead (2:63).

Casting our eyes elsewhere, we may observe a contrast between passive and armed resistance which is drawn in the subsections. The pertinent verses are 2:37 (1.D) and 3:59 (1.D′).

> [Many who were seeking righteousness and justice] said, "Let us all die in our innocence (ἀποθάνωμεν πάντες ἐν τῇ ἁπλότητι ἡμῶν); heaven and earth testify for us that you are killing us unjustly." (2:37)

> [Judas said:] "It is better for us to die in battle (κρεῖσσον ἡμᾶς ἀποθανεῖν ἐν τῷ πολέμῳ) than to see the misfortunes of our nation and of the sanctuary." (3:59)

Another connection between 1.D and 1.D′ comes through their emphases on the Jewish ancestors. First, in 1.D, at the beginning of his dying words to his sons, Mattathias tells them: "Remember the deeds of our ancestors (μνήσθητε τῶν πατέρων ἡμῶν τὰ ἔργα), which they did in their generations; and you will receive great honor and an everlasting name" (2:51). He then proceeds, in 2:52–60, to mention Abraham, Joseph, Phinehas, Joshua, Caleb, David, Elijah, Hananiah, Azariah, Mishael, and Daniel. Correspondingly, in 1.D′, when Judas is about to lead the Jews into battle against the Greek commander Gorgias, he tells them: "Remember how our ancestors were saved (μνήσθητε ὡς ἐσώθησαν οἱ πατέρες ἡμῶν) at the Red Sea, when Pharaoh with his forces pursued them" (4:9). Similarly, before facing Lysias, Judas "prayed, saying, 'Blessed are you, O Savior of Israel, who crushed the attack of the mighty warrior by the hand of your servant David, and gave the camp of the Philistines into the hands of Jonathan son of Saul, and of the man who carried his armor'" (4:30).[16] Second, in 1.D Mattathias twice speaks (2:20 and 2:50) of the "covenant of our ancestors (διαθήκη/διαθήκης πατέρων ἡμῶν)." The same wording appears in 1.D′ at 4:10, when Judas tells his soldiers: "Let us cry to Heaven, to see whether he will favor us and remember his covenant with our ancestors (διαθήκης πατέρων) and crush this army before us today." This expression only occurs in 1 Maccabees these three times. Once more, such correspondences seem contrived.[17]

[16] Cf. 1 Sam 14:1–17.

[17] This claim is bolstered by observing that Judas' prayer at 4:30–33 (which mentions, as we have just seen, David, Jonathan, and Saul) is relatively lengthy, while the description of the battle which follows is brief (4:34). The emphasis falls, then, on Judas' words with their remembrance of the ancestors.

Summary of Symmetries for Section One

Before we turn to consider section two, let us pause to review the symmetries between the paired subsections of section one that we have observed in this chapter, as well as in the preceding pages. Summary charts follow.

1.A	1.A′
• Alexander the Great is described as the son of Philip, a Macedonian, and king of Greece	• Alexander the Great is described as the son of Philip, a Macedonian, and king of the Greeks
• Alexander dies after falling on a bed, knowing that he would die, and summoning his retainers	• Antiochus IV dies after falling on a bed, thinking that he would die, and summoning his Friends

1.B	1.B′
• Renegade Jews want to make a covenant with the Gentiles all around	• The Gentiles all around want to annihilate the Jews
• Renegade Jews join with the Gentiles around them	• Faithful Jews defeat the Gentiles around them

1.C	1.C′
• The temple is plundered	• Temple paraphernalia are restored
• The altar is desecrated	• A new altar is dedicated
• Greeks fortify the City of David	• Jews fortify Mount Zion
• Great wrath has come upon Israel	• There is great joy among the Jews

1.D	1.D′
• Mattathias says it is a time of "wrathful anger"	• Antiochus has "wrathful anger"
• Mattathias says "of the words of a 'sinful man' be not afraid"	• Antiochus (a "sinful root") orders the annihilation of the Jews
• Mattathias and his sons tear their clothes and put on sackcloth	• Judas and his followers tear their clothes and put on sackcloth
• Some Jews say "let us die in our innocence"	• Judas says that "it is better to die in battle"
• Mattathias says to "remember the deeds of the ancestors" and the "covenant of our ancestors"	• Judas recalls Jewish ancestors before battles and mentions the "covenant with our ancestors"

2.AA′

In the preceding chapter I demonstrated that 2.A (6:18–7:50) and 2.A′ (12:24–14:15) each have a coherent theme: in 2.A there are three military campaigns against Judas and his followers that are instigated by "godless" entities, and in 2.A′ we encounter Simon's rise to power. These themes appear to have nothing in common, and thus a direct connection between 2.A and 2.A′ is not readily apparent. Further examination suggests, however, that 2.AA′ are indeed linked by symmetries.

To begin with, in each subsection there is a major turn of events as the Jews acquire a significant freedom. In 2.A Antiochus V makes peace with the Jews, upon the recommendation of Lysias (6:58–60). In the process, the Jews are granted freedom of religion, for Lysias counsels: "Let us agree to let them live by their laws as they did before" (6:59). In 2.A′ the Jews obtain political freedom from Demetrius II, who writes in a letter to Simon: "We are ready to make a general peace with you" (13:37). Thus, the Jews achieve independence.[18]

[18] While Simon gained virtual autonomy, complete independence did not come until John Hyrcanus' day, after the death of Antiochus VII. Nevertheless, it is clear that 1 Maccabees pre-

This thematic linkage is supported by other connections between 2.A and 2.A′. For instance, the first of the five sons of Mattathias to die is Eleazar Avaran, who is crushed by an elephant in 2.A at 6:46. In 2.A′ Simon becomes the last of the brothers to survive when Jonathan is killed. This matter is highlighted in 2.A′ when Simon states: "All my brothers have perished for the sake of Israel, and I alone am left" (13:4).

A further similarity between 2.A and 2.A′ is how each subsection underscores the idea that the enemies of the faithful Jews are deceitful and treacherous. To be sure, it is not surprising to find such a notion expressed in 1 Maccabees.[19] What I wish to point out, however, is the concentration of references to deceit in 2.AA′. In the light of the material to follow, it seems as though one verse in 2.A sounds a leitmotif for 2.AA′. In 7:18, after Alcimus has slaughtered some pious Jews (Hasideans), we are told that the people cry out, saying: "There is no truth or justice in them, for they have violated the agreement and the oath that they swore." Indeed, virtually every enemy figure in 2.AA′ is shown to be deceitful.

(1) In 6:61 Antiochus V gives the Jews his oath and, on this condition, the Jews evacuate a stronghold. But in 6:62 the king breaks his oath.

(2) In 7:10 Bacchides sends messengers to Judas and his brothers, "with peaceable but treacherous (μετὰ δόλου) words."[20]

(3) In 7:15–16 Alcimus speaks peaceably to the Hasideans and swears to them that he will not seek to injure them. In 7:17, however, he seizes sixty of the Hasideans and has them killed.

(4) In 7:27–28 Nicanor treacherously (μετὰ δόλου) sends Judas a peaceable message. He states: "Let there be no fighting between you and me; I shall come with a few men (ἀνδράσιν ὀλίγοις) to see you face to face in peace." We learn in 7:29, however, that "the enemy were preparing to kidnap

---

sents the case that independence came under Simon. Cf. 1 Macc 13:41–42: "In the one hundred seventieth year the yoke of the Gentiles was removed from Israel, and the people began to write in their documents and contracts, 'In the first year of Simon the great high priest and commander and leader of the Jews.'"

[19] Indeed, the tone is set early on in the book:

> [Antiochus IV] sent to the cities of Judah a chief collector of tribute, and he came to Jerusalem with a large force. Deceitfully he spoke peaceable words to them, and they believed him; but he suddenly fell upon the city, dealt it a severe blow, and destroyed many people of Israel. (1:29–30)

[20] The term δόλος ("deceit") occurs ten times in 1 Maccabees (1:30; 7:10, 27, 30; 8:28; 11:1; 13:17, 31; 16:13, 15). As may be seen, half of these appearances are in 2.AA′ (7:10, 27, 30; 13:17, 31).

Judas." When it was clear to Judas in 7:30 that Nicanor had come to him with treacherous intent (μετὰ δόλου), he refused to meet with him.

(5) The preceding cases concern 2.A. In 2.A′ the main enemy is Trypho. We find two instances where his deceitfulness with Jews is manifest.[21] First, in 12:44–48 an event occurs which is similar to that which we have just seen in 7:27–30. In 12:45 Trypho tells Jonathan to meet him with a few men (ἄνδρας ὀλίγους), and he will hand over Ptolemais to the Jews, and will "turn around and go home." Jonathan trusts Trypho, but when he enters Ptolemais, the gates are closed and he and his men are seized (12:46–48). Second, after capturing Jonathan, Trypho demands, in return for Jonathan's release, one hundred talents of silver from Simon, as well as two hostages (13:16). We are told in 13:17 that Simon knew Trypho's envoys were "speaking deceitfully (δόλῳ)," but he acquiesced nevertheless. In 13:19, however, we learn that "Trypho broke his word" and did not release Jonathan.

On balance, then, there are indeed impressive connections between 2.A and 2.A′. Especially striking is the parallel between the acquisition of religious freedom in 2.A and the acquisition of political freedom in 2.A′.[22]

2.BB′

In 2.B (8:1–32) a history of Rome is presented, which is followed by an account of a Jewish mission to Rome that leads to a treaty between the Jews and the Romans. In 2.B′ (12:1–23) a second Jewish mission is sent to Rome

[21] He is also deceitful with a fellow Greek: "Trypho dealt treacherously (δόλῳ) with the young King Antiochus [V]; he killed him" (13:31).

[22] It is important to note that 1 Maccabees skips over the amnesty that seems to have been offered to the Jews in 164 BCE (cf. 2 Macc 11:18–21, 27–33). Often, scholars assert that this is because the author had no desire to credit the high priest, Menelaus, with securing the end of the persecution, the negotiations presumably having excluded Judas. For instance, Doran (*The First Book of Maccabees*, 91) remarks, concerning 1 Macc 6:59: "Peace negotiations had already been initiated during the reign of Antiochus IV. No mention is made of these overtures in 1 Maccabees, however, possibly because they involved Jewish groups other than the Maccabees." The weakness of this argument is that the Hasmonean figures are not mentioned in regard to the negotiations in 162 with Antiochus V and Lysias, either. (Cf. 6:60: "The speech [of Lysias] pleased the king and the commanders, and he sent to *the Jews* [πρὸς αὐτοὺς] an offer of peace, and *they accepted it* [ἐπεδέξαντο].") Thus, silence concerning the Hasmoneans does not seem to offer a sufficient explanation for the lack of a reference in 1 Maccabees to the amnesty of 164. In this light, we should observe that by not mentioning the amnesty, which would appear in section one, 1 Maccabees has the first peace negotiations between the Jews and the Seleucids take place later, in 2.A, and the acquisition of peace in 2.A thereby balances the acquisition of independence in 2.A′.

to confirm and renew the treaty made in 1 Maccabees 8, and also Jewish relations with the Spartans are related.

The reader will recall from my discussion in chapter two above that each of these subsections interrupts a sequence of military campaigns. This situation is important, given scholarly attitudes toward such interruptions elsewhere in studies of structure.[23] M. Fishbane, for instance, in commenting about the Jacob Cycle, writes:

> *Genesis 26* [is] anamolous in the present context . . . the symmetrical episode . . . in *Genesis 34* . . . is also without visible relationship to its surrounding context. . . . The symmetry between Genesis 26 and 34, together with their parallel functions as interludes . . . preclude any assumption of a haphazard editorial arrangement.[24]

In order to appreciate the extensive symmetry between 2.B and 2.B′, consider the following material.

8:17–20	12:1–3
	καὶ εἶδεν Ιωναθαν ὅτι ὁ καιρὸς αὐτῷ συνεργεῖ,
καὶ ἐπελέξεν Ιουδας τὸν Εὐπόλεμον υἱὸν Ιωαννου τοῦ Ακκως καὶ Ἰάσονα υἱὸν Ελεαζαρου,	καὶ ἐπελέξεν ἄνδρας
καὶ ἀπέστειλεν αὐτοὺς εἰς Ῥώμην στῆσαι αὐτοῖς φιλίαν καὶ συμμαχίαν καὶ τοῦ ἆραι τὸν ζυγὸν ἀπ᾽ αὐτῶν, ὅτι εἶδον τὴν βασιλείαν τῶν Ἑλλήνων καταδουλουμένους τὸν Ισραηλ δουλείαν	καὶ ἀπέστειλεν εἰς Ῥώμην στῆσαι καὶ ἀνανεώσασθαι τὴν πρὸς αὐτοὺς φιλίαν

[23] For example, M. Brettler ("The Structure of 1 Kings 1–11," *JSOT* 49 [1991] 88–89) observes that "features such as unexpected, problematic repetitions, or material which seems chronologically or thematically misplaced . . . suggest that an author/editor was structuring the material with a particular purpose in mind."

[24] M. Fishbane, *Text and Texture* (New York: Schocken, 1979) 46–47. For a convenient survey of the Jacob Cycle, with bibliography, see S. D. Walters, "Jacob Narrative," *ABD* 3. 599–608.

	καὶ πρὸς Σπαρτιάτας καὶ τόπους ἑτέρους ἀπέστειλεν ἐπιστολὰς κατὰ ταῦτα
καὶ ἐπορεύθησαν εἰς Ῥώμην– καὶ ἡ ὁδὸς πολλὴ σφόδρα–	καὶ ἐπορεύθησαν εἰς Ῥώμην
καὶ εἰσήλθοσαν εἰς τὸ βουλευτήριον	καὶ εἰσῆλθον εἰς τὸ βουλευτήριον
καὶ ἀπεκρίθησαν καὶ εἶπον Ἰούδας ὁ καὶ Μακκαβαῖος καὶ οἱ ἀδελφοὶ αὐτοῦ	καὶ εἶπαν Ιωναθαν ὁ ἀρχιερεὺς
καὶ τὸ πλῆθος τῶν Ἰουδαίων ἀπέστειλαν ἡμᾶς πρὸς ὑμᾶς στῆσαι μεθ' ὑμῶν συμμαχίαν καὶ εἰρήνην καὶ γραφῆναι ἡμᾶς συμμάχους καὶ φίλους ὑμῶν	καὶ τὸ ἔθνος τῶν Ιουδαίων ἀπέστειλεν ἡμᾶς ἀνανεώσασθαι τὴν φιλίαν αὐτοῖς καὶ τὴν συμμαχίαν κατὰ τὸ πρότερον
	Now when Jonathan saw that the time was favorable for him,
So Judas chose Eupolemus son of John son of Accos, and Jason son of Eleazar,	he chose men
and sent them to Rome, to establish friendship and alliance, and to free themselves from the yoke; for they saw that the kingdom of the Greeks was enslaving Israel completely.	and sent them to Rome to confirm and renew the friendship with them.
	He also sent letters to the same effect to the Spartans and to other places.
They went to Rome, a very long journey;	So they went to Rome
and they entered the senate chamber	and entered the senate chamber
and spoke as follows: "Judas, who is also called	and said, "The high priest Jonathan

Maccabeus, and his brothers
and the people of the Jews
have sent us to you to establish
alliance and peace with you,
so that we may be enrolled as
your allies and friends."

and the Jewish nation
have sent us to renew
the former friendship
and alliance with them."

It is readily apparent that there is a strong connectedness between 2.B and 2.B′.

2.CC′

We have seen previously that both 2.C and 2.C′ are concerned with Jonathan acquiring and/or maintaining his station as a "mighty one" in the Seleucid empire. I will now present a number of additional symmetries between 2.C and 2.C′.

(1) Several letters written to Jonathan and/or the Jews are mentioned in the subsections: in 2.C Demetrius I writes at 10:3–6 and 10:25–45, and Alexander Balas at 10:18–20 and 10:59; in 2.C′ Apollonius writes at 10:70–73, Demetrius II at 11:22, 11:30–37, and 11:42–43, and Antiochus VI at 11:57.[25] I would like to focus on three of the letters written by kings named Demetrius: the lengthy letter of Demetrius I to the Jews in 2.C (10:25–45), and two of the letters of Demetrius II to Jonathan in 2.C′ (11:30–37 and 11:42–43). In the following, we will observe three areas of specific similarity among these letters.

First, we find analogous references to exemptions for the Jews.

καὶ νῦν ἀπολύω ὑμᾶς καὶ ἀφίημι πάντας τοὺς Ἰουδαίους ἀπὸ τῶν φόρων καὶ τῆς τιμῆς τοῦ ἁλὸς καὶ ἀπὸ τῶν στεφάνων . . . καὶ Ιερουσαλημ ἤτω ἁγία καὶ ἀφειμένη καὶ τὰ ὅρια αὐτῆς, αἱ δεκάται καὶ τὰ τέλη (10:29, 31)

I [sc. Demetrius I] now free you and exempt all the Jews from payment of tribute and salt tax and crown levies . . . Jerusalem and its environs, its tithes and its revenues, shall be holy and free from tax.

[25] Indeed, letters abound in 2.CC′. In addition to those described in the text above, the following letters are either quoted or alluded to: Bacchides to his allies (9:60); Alexander Balas to Ptolemy VI (10:52–54); Ptolemy to Alexander (10:55–56); and Ptolemy to Demetrius II (11:9–10).

> καὶ τὰ ἄλλα τὰ ἀνήκοντα ἡμῖν ἀπὸ τοῦ νῦν <u>τῶν δεκατῶν καὶ τῶν τελῶν</u> τῶν ἀνηκόντων ἡμῖν καὶ τὰς <u>τοῦ ἁλὸς</u> λίμνας καὶ τοὺς ἀνήκοντας ἡμῖν <u>στεφάνους,</u> πάντα ἐπαρκέσομεν αὐτοῖς (11:35)
>
> And the other payments henceforth due to us [sc. Demetrius II] of the tithes, and the taxes due to us, and the salt pits and the crown taxes due to us—from all these we shall grant them release.

Second, there are comparable promises to give three districts in Samaria to the Jews.

> <u>καὶ τοὺς τρεῖς νομοὺς</u> τοὺς προστεθέντας <u>τῇ Ἰουδαίᾳ ἀπὸ τῆς χώρας Σαμαρείας</u> προστεθήτω <u>τῇ Ἰουδαίᾳ</u> πρὸς τὸ λογισθῆναι τοῦ γενέσθαι ὑφ' ἕνα τοῦ μὴ ὑπακοῦσαι ἄλλης ἐξουσίας ἀλλ' ἢ τοῦ ἀρχιερέως (10:38)
>
> As for the three districts that have been added to Judea from the country of Samaria, let them be annexed to Judea so that they may be considered to be under one ruler and obey no other authority than the high priest.
>
> ἑστάκαμεν αὐτοῖς τά τε ὅρια <u>τῆς Ἰουδαίας καὶ τοὺς τρεῖς νομοὺς</u> Αφαιρεμα καὶ Λυδδα καὶ Ῥαμαθαιμ· προσετέθησαν <u>τῇ Ἰουδαίᾳ ἀπὸ τῆς Σαμαρίτιδος</u> καὶ πάντα τὰ συγκυροῦντα αὐτοῖς (11:34)
>
> We have confirmed as their possession both the territory of Judea and the three districts of Aphairema and Lydda and Rathamin; the latter, with all the region bordering them, were added to Judea from Samaria.

Third, each king promises to relinquish the citadel.

> I [sc. Demetrius I] release also my control of the citadel in Jerusalem (τῆς ἄκρας τῆς ἐν Ιερουσαλημ) and give it to the high priest, so that he may station in it men of his own choice to guard it. (10:32)
>
> Now Jonathan sent to King Demetrius [II] the request that he remove the troops of the citadel from Jerusalem (τῆς ἄκρας ἐξ Ιερουσαλημ), and the troops in the strongholds; for they kept fighting against Israel. And Demetrius sent this message back to Jonathan: "Not only will I do these things for you and your nation, but I will confer great honor on you and your nation, if I find an opportunity." (11:41–42)

What makes these resemblances all the more remarkable is that the letter from Demetrius I which is quoted at such length from 10:25 to 10:45 is immediately rejected by the Jews at 10:46! Why, then, does this letter appear in such detail?[26] Given the Jewish rejection of the letter, we might reasonably expect a simple summary of it or a mere acknowledgment that such a letter was sent.[27] It is tempting to find structural considerations at work here. As we have seen, the vocabulary and concepts of the letter are mirrored in certain letters in 1 Maccabees 11 (11:30–37 and 11:42–43). Thus, by providing the text of the letter the narrative supplies a link between 2.C and 2.C′.

(2) In each subsection Jonathan is elevated in rank by a foreign king. Jonathan is appointed to the high priesthood by Alexander Balas in 2.C (10:20), and is later confirmed in the position in 2.C′ by Demetrius II (11:27) and Antiochus VI (11:57). He becomes Alexander's Friend in 2.C at 10:20, and Antiochus' Friend in 2.C′ at 11:57. Further, he is enrolled among Alexander's chief Friends in 2.C at 10:65, and is reckoned among Demetrius' chief Friends in 2.C′ at 11:27. These are the only two appearances of the term "chief (or first) Friends" (πρώτων φίλων) in 1 Maccabees. Finally, Jonathan is given permission to wear purple by Alexander in 2.C at 10:20 and 10:62, and by Antiochus in 2.C′ at 11:58.[28]

(3) In both subsections, there is an account of a battle, followed by the death of royalty, after which a king asserts his power. In 2.C Alexander Balas meets Demetrius I in battle at 10:48–49. Demetrius dies at 10:50, and Alexander then sends ambassadors to Ptolemy VI to declare that he has defeated Demetrius and established his rule (10:51–54). In 2.C′, having had a falling out, Alexander and Ptolemy meet in battle at 11:15. Both kings die in the aftermath of the battle (11:17–18), and, in 11:19, Demetrius II claims the throne.

(4) In each subsection, Ptolemy VI gives away his daughter, Cleopatra Thea, in marriage. As we have just seen, in 2.C, after having defeated Demetrius I, Alexander Balas sent a message to Ptolemy VI. In 10:54, as part of this message, Alexander addressed the following to Ptolemy: "Give me now your daughter as my wife, and I will become your son-in-law." Ptolemy subsequently met with Alexander at Ptolemais "and gave him his daughter Cleopatra in marriage" (10:58). In 2.C′, however, Ptolemy—now angry with Alexander—sends envoys to Demetrius II saying, "Let us make a covenant

[26] Goldstein (*I Maccabees*, 414) remarks about the "strange impression created by quoting Demetrius' sweeping concessions only to record that the Jews rejected them."

[27] Cf. the brevity with which the other letters of 2.CC′ are handled: 9:60; 10:3–6; 10:18–20; 10:52–54; 10:55–56; 10:59; 10:70–73; 11:9–10; 11:22; 11:30–37; 11:42–43; 11:57.

[28] For a discussion of the ranks associated with the members of the Seleucid royal court, as well as their privileges, see Bickerman, *Institutions*, 40–50.

with each other and I will give you my daughter *who was Alexander's wife*" (11:9), and we are told that Cleopatra did indeed marry Demetrius (cf. 11:12). Note how the highlighted words of 11:9 in 2.C′ provide a bridge back to 2.C.

(5) Finally, a strong connection between 2.C and 2.C′ comes through their similar accounts of visits by Jonathan to Ptolemais to meet with royalty (10:59–66 and 11:20–37). We have already touched on these episodes in the preceding chapters. At this point, let us observe the close verbal relations between the following sets of verses.

10:60–61	11:24–25
καὶ ἐπορεύθη μετὰ δόξης	
εἰς Πτολεμαΐδα καὶ ἀπήντησε	
τοῖς δυσὶ βασιλεῦσι	
καὶ ἔδωκεν αὐτοῖς	καὶ λαβὼν
ἀργύριον καὶ χρυσίον	ἀργύριον καὶ χρυσίον
	καὶ ἱματισμὸν
καὶ τοῖς φίλοις αὐτῶν	
καὶ δόματα πολλὰ	καὶ ἕτερα ξένια πλείονα
	καὶ ἐπορεύθη πρὸς τὸν
	βασιλέα εἰς Πτολεμαΐδα
καὶ εὗρε χάριν	καὶ εὗρε χάριν
ἐνώπιον αὐτῶν	ἐναντίον αὐτοῦ
καὶ ἐπισυνήχθησαν ἐπ᾽ αὐτὸν	
ἄνδρες λοιμοὶ ἐξ Ισραηλ	
ἄνδρες παράνομοι	
ἐντυχεῖν	καὶ ἐνετύγχανον
κατ᾽ αὐτοῦ	κατ᾽ αὐτοῦ
	τινες ἄνομοι τῶν ἐκ τοῦ ἔθνους
So [Jonathan]	
went with pomp	
to Ptolemais and met	
the two kings;	
he gave them	And taking
silver and gold	silver and gold
	and clothing

as well as to their Friends	
and many gifts,	and many other gifts
	[Jonathan] went to
	the king at Ptolemais
and found favor	and found favor
with them.	with him.
There gathered against	
[Jonathan]	
a group of lawless men	And certain lawless men
from Israel,	of his nation
renegades,	
to accuse him.	accused [Jonathan].

In sum, it is clear that several symmetries establish cohesive ties between 2.C and 2.C′.

Summary of Symmetries for Section Two

The following charts summarize the symmetries that we have observed between the paired subsections of section two.

2.A	**2.A′**
• The Jews acquire freedom of religion	• The Jews acquire political freedom
• The first of Mattathias' five sons to die is Eleazar	• The last of Mattathias' five sons to survive is Simon
• The enemies of the Jews are deceitful	• Trypho, an enemy of the Jews, is deceitful

2.B	**2.B′**
• A Jewish mission goes to Rome to establish an alliance	• A second Jewish mission goes to Rome to renew the alliance

2.C	2.C′
• The Jews receive a letter from Demetrius I	• Jonathan receives two letters from Demetrius II
• Jonathan is elevated in rank by a foreign king	• Jonathan is elevated in rank by foreign kings
• Following a battle and the death of royalty, a king asserts his power	• Following a battle and the death of royalty, a king asserts his power
• Cleopatra Thea marries Alexander Balas	• Cleopatra Thea marries Demetrius II
• Jonathan visits royalty at Ptolemais	• Jonathan visits royalty at Ptolemais

Conclusion

The observations made in this chapter serve to secure the theory of the architecture of 1 Maccabees that was proposed in the previous chapter. While the summary charts I have provided emphasize thematic symmetries between the various paired subsections, it is important to recall that we have also observed verbal symmetries, since such types of evidence serve to reinforce one another.[29] Given all of the evidence we have reviewed, it is reasonable to assert that 1 Macc 1:1–14:15 is arranged in two chiastic structures: section one (1:1–6:17) and section two (6:18–14:15).

In symmetrical scenes or acts in biblical narratives we may observe three fundamental relationships: parallel, intensificatory-parallel, and contrastive.[30] The paired subsections in the chiastic structures of 1 Maccabees display all three of these relationship patterns. 2.BB′ exemplifies a parallel relationship, especially in the closeness of the wording that describes the Jewish diplomatic missions to Rome. Similarly, we have observed a number of parallel features between 2.C and 2.C′, including the episodes of Jonathan

[29] Cf. Bar-Efrat, "Analysis of Structure," 172.

[30] See Bar-Efrat, *Narrative Art*, 98–111.

visiting royalty in Ptolemais. In the depiction of the death of Antiochus IV in 1.A′ we may see an intensification of the parallel description of the death of Alexander the Great in 1.A, since Antiochus' death process is elongated by comparison to that of Alexander and is punctuated by grief. Some of the paired subsections are contrastive in some fashion. Consider the following examples: (1) lawless Jews seek a relationship with Gentiles in 1.B, but faithful Jews defeat Gentiles who have attacked them in 1.B′; and (2) the temple is robbed and desecrated in 1.C, but it is restored and rededicated in 1.C′.

In the following chapter I will explore the thematic highlighting performed by the chiastic structures of sections one and two.

CHAPTER 6

Major Themes in Sections One and Two (1:1–14:15)

Butterworth suggests that, having discovered the structure of a biblical work, one should attempt to determine its purpose.[1] I will now take up the issue of meaning in the chiastic structures of sections one and two. In doing so, we come face to face with a major issue of scholarly debate: how far should/may we go in assigning authorial intent?

On the one hand, Muilenburg claimed that the proper articulation of form "will reveal to us the texture and fabric of the writer's thought, not only what it is that he thinks, but as he thinks it."[2] In other words, he asserted that we can discover an author's intention through rhetorical analysis.

Person, however, has criticized Butterworth for the latter's goal of finding methods to determine whether an apparent structure was actually planned by an author or editor. According to Person, this goal

> is problematic for it is based upon an extremely individualistic understanding of literary artistry that does not take into account traditional influences upon any writer. Traditional influences are sometimes unrecognized by writers because they are simply taken for granted; therefore, writers will not always be conscious of all of the structural devices they are using.[3]

[1] Cf. item number 10 on Boda's list in chapter one.

[2] Muilenburg, "Form Criticism and Beyond," 7.

[3] Person, review of Butterworth, 134. D. J. Clark ("Criteria for Identifying Chiasm," *Linguistica Biblica* 35 [1975] 71–72) makes a similar argument (author's own emphasis).

> The human brain . . . habitually works in patterns of the most amazing complexity, even when the owner is competely unaware of this. For an example, one need look no further

To be sure, authors are sometimes taken aback when they discover things in their compositions that they did not consciously intend, and therefore it is reasonable to conclude that authorial intention accounts for only a part, and not the whole, of a text's meaning.[4] This understanding differs from the positions of Muilenburg and Butterworth. Nevertheless, it still allows for the discovery of meaning behind structure, for, while we may quibble over the extent of the author's intention behind the meaning of a given structure, we can acknowledge that some meaning is present.[5]

To sum up, in this chapter I will concentrate on meaning in the chiastic structures that I have identified in sections one and two of 1 Maccabees, but I will not be overly concerned with the degree of authorial intention behind meaning. Given the extent of the formal symmetries connecting paired subsections in the structures, it seems reasonable to presume some degree of authorial intention. Yet, I acknowledge that there may be some meaning that is not in keeping with what the author(s) of 1 Maccabees intended. As Bar-Efrat concludes: "It makes no difference if [an] author used the techniques consciously or not, the crucial point is what formal methods are actually present in the work, what they contribute and how they function."[6]

Analysis of Themes in 1.E

An appropriate starting point for my analysis of meaning in sections one and two of 1 Maccabees is the central subsection of section one, for, as was

> than the sound patterns of the English language, used every day correctly but unknowingly by millions of linguistically naive native speakers. Such patterns exist in the morphological and syntactic aspects of language also, and there is no *a priori* reason why they should not occur at a higher, literary or "discourse" level. That they do in fact so occur can be readily verified by examining ordinary mundane correspondence. To suggest that such patterning is subconscious is not at all to say that it is accidental. Rather is it likely to be the response to a host of *stimuli* arising from a complex of cultural conditioning and individual psychology.

[4] I am drawing in this paragraph upon Trible, *Rhetorical Criticism*, 96–97.

[5] Cf. Trible (*Rhetorical Criticism*, 230), who writes about recognizing signs of intentionality in Jonah, without having to determine their specific point of origin:

> We do not know the intention of the flesh-and-blood author of Jonah, but we can discern signals of intentionality in the text. Whether they come from the actual author, the implied author, the implied reader, or interaction between the text and the actual reader remains a moot proposition.

[6] Bar-Efrat, *Narrative Art*, 10–11.

discussed in chapter one above, we should investigate whether the center of a chiastic structure in a narrative setting is in any way highlighting material. Let us observe what is accented by 1.E (3:1–26) in 1 Maccabees.[7] First, there is a significant shift in the narrative. In 3:1, at the outset of the subsection, Judas emerges as the leader of the Jewish revolt, following the death of Mattathias. In the next verse we learn that "all his brothers" helped Judas (3:2). Together, they defeat the first Seleucid expeditions against them, led by Apollonius and Seron (3:10–11, 13–24). At the end of the subsection we read: "Then Judas and his brothers began to be feared, and terror fell on the Gentiles all around them" (3:25).

Thus, this subsection marks the beginning of the career of Judas and his brothers, a grouping that is obviously of importance in the book as a whole. Indeed, as we have seen, the standard scholarly position is that 1 Maccabees has four main parts: first an introduction, and then three separate segments for the careers, in turn, of Judas, Jonathan, and Simon. While it is clear that I do not share this notion, and that I divide the book along different lines, I agree that Judas and his brothers take center stage in 1 Maccabees. We may speak, therefore, of a pro-Hasmonean advocacy in the book.[8]

There is also a second important theme in 1.E that is a theological focus of 1 Maccabees. When the Jewish forces are opposed by Seron they find themselves far outnumbered (cf. 3:13–17) and ask: "How can we, few as we are, fight against so great and so strong a multitude?" (3:17). Judas replies: "It is

[7] It should be realized that 1.E is especially important since section two lacks a central subsection.

[8] This has been a popular notion among scholars since A. Geiger (*Urschrift und Übersetzungen der Bibel* [1857; reprinted, Frankfurt/Main: Madda, 1928] 206) asserted that the author of 1 Maccabees was an official historian for the Hasmonean dynasty. Goldstein (*I Maccabees*, 588) is especially emphatic concerning the pro-Hasmonean stance of 1 Maccabees, remarking that the "thesis" of the author is "that God had chosen the Hasmonean dynasty to lead Israel." According to S. Schwartz ("Israel and the Nations Roundabout: 1 Maccabees and the Hasmonean Expansion," *JJS* 42 [1991] 17 n. 3), "in this century only Robert Pfeiffer, *A History of New Testament Times with an Introduction to the Apocrypha* (New York, 1949), p. 493, has argued that promotion of the Hasmonean dynasty was not an important part of 1 Macc.'s agenda." But cf. now also Doran (*The First Book of Maccabees*, 22):

> I would suggest that one should look more carefully at the assumption that the work is pro-Hasmonean. . . . There is [a] contrast between the utopian picture of Roman government in chapter 8 and the one-man rule imposed by Simon (14:41–45). Therefore, 1 Maccabees may be seen as a critique of the developments that had taken place under Hyrcanus and his successors.

easy for many to be hemmed in by few, for in the sight of Heaven there is no difference between saving by many or by few. It is not on the size of the army that victory in battle depends, but strength comes from Heaven" (3:18–19).[9]

These words highlight the idea that God assists the Jews, a theme recognized by some scholars as having importance in the book, alongside the notion that the Jews must–to some degree–take matters into their own hands. For example, according to Oesterley:

> The writer [of 1 Maccabees] is very far from being wanting in religious belief and feeling; his conviction of the existence of an all-seeing Providence who helps those who are worthy comes out strongly . . . but he evidently has an almost equally strong belief in the truth expressed in the modern proverb, that "God helps those who help themselves."[10]

This idea of God helping those who help themselves should be understood within the ancient context. To some modern sensibilities, the notion represents self-sufficiency. But this is clearly not the case in 1 Maccabees. Indeed, in 3:22 Judas asserts, concerning divine assistance, that "He himself will crush them before us (αὐτὸς συντρίψει αὐτοὺς πρὸ προσώπου ἡμῶν)."[11] Since these words refer to Jewish military action and not to any miraculous intervention (as in 2 Macc 3:24–28), we may refer to this belief as double causality. According to this understanding, events occur because of both human and divine causes, and "God's actions are not separate from those of humanity . . . but are intertwined with them."[12]

We find significant echoes of Judas' words in 3:22 throughout sections one and two. We will focus on the use of the verb συντρίβω ("to crush"), which appears, in addition to 3:22, twenty-two other times in 1 Maccabees.[13] The following are the most important occurrences, given our present topic.

(1) In 3:23, immediately following Judas' utterance that God would "crush" the enemy before the Jews, that indeed transpires: "When [Judas] finished speaking, he rushed suddenly against Seron and his army, and they

[9] Cf. Deut 20:1–4 and 1 Sam 14:6.

[10] Oesterley, "The First Book of Maccabees," 61.

[11] Note how the personal pronoun adds emphasis.

[12] Bar-Efrat, *Narrative Art*, 28. On this notion, see also D. Arenhoevel, *Die Theokratie nach dem 1. und 2. Makkabäer* (Mainz: Matthias Grünewald, 1967) 36, and Y. Amit, "The Dual Causality Principle and its Effects on Biblical Literature," *VT* 37 (1987) 385–400.

[13] 3:23; 4:10, 14, 30, 36; 5:7, 21, 43; 7:42, 43; 8:4, 5, 6; 9:7, 15, 16, 68; 10:52, 53, 82; 13:51; 14:13.

were crushed before him (καὶ συνετρίβη Σήρων καὶ ἡ παρεμβολὴ αὐτοῦ ἐνώπιον αὐτοῦ)."[14]

(2) In 4:10 Judas is facing troops led by Gorgias. Judas tells his own soldiers: "And now, let us cry to Heaven, to see whether he will favor us and remember his covenant with our ancestors and crush this army before us today (καὶ συντρίψει τὴν παρεμβολὴν ταύτην κατὰ πρόσωπον ἡμῶν σήμερον)." In the subsequent battle "the Gentiles were crushed (συνετρίβησαν) and fled" (4:14).

(3) A force led by Lysias comes against Judas and his troops in 4:28–29. In 4:30 we read: "When [Judas] saw that their army was strong, he prayed, saying, 'Blessed are you, O Savior of Israel, who crushed (ὁ συντρίψας) the attack of the mighty warrior by the hand of your servant David. . . .'"

(4) In the wake of their various victories, Judas and his brothers prepare to liberate the temple: "Then Judas and his brothers said, 'See, our enemies are crushed (συνετρίβησαν); let us go up to cleanse the sanctuary and dedicate it'" (4:36).

(5) Three times, in the descriptions of the expeditions against local Gentiles in 1 Maccabees 5, we hear of Gentiles being "crushed" before the Jews. First, in 5:7, Judas confronts the Ammonites: "He engaged in many battles with them, and they were crushed before him (καὶ συνετρίβησαν πρὸ προσώπου αὐτοῦ); he struck them down." Second, according to 5:21, Simon "went to Galilee and fought many battles against the Gentiles, and the Gentiles were crushed before him (καὶ συνετρίβη τὰ ἔθνη ἀπὸ προσώπου αὐτοῦ)." Finally, 5:43 tells us that Judas led a charge against some Gentiles and "they were crushed before him (συνετρίβησαν πρὸ προσώπου αὐτῶν)."

(6) In 7:42 we find Judas praying before confronting the army of Nicanor. He requests: "So also crush this army before us today (σύντριψον τὴν παρεμβολὴν ταύτην ἐνώπιον ἡμῶν σήμερον)." In the next verse we are told: "So the armies met in battle on the thirteenth day of the month of Adar. The army of Nicanor was crushed (συνετρίβη), and he himself was the first to fall in the battle."

(7) Beginning with 9:13, Judas and his men do battle against the forces of Bacchides. According to the account Judas spotted that Bacchides and the strength of his army were on the right wing, so he led his forces to that side. We are then told that the Jews "crushed (συνετρίβη) the right wing, and

[14] Observe the passive form of συντρίβω here and often in what follows, which emphasizes divine action.

[Judas] pursued them as far as Mount Azotus. When those on the left wing saw that the right wing was crushed (συνετρίβη), they turned and followed close behind Judas and his men" (9:15–16).[15] As we have seen previously, Judas was killed in the ensuing conflict. He was avenged to some degree, however, for according to 9:68 Simon and his troops later "fought with Bacchides, and he was crushed (συνετρίβη) by them."

(8) Simon is also successful in 10:82, when facing some troops led by Apollonius: "Then Simon brought forward his force and engaged the phalanx in battle (for the cavalry was exhausted); they were crushed (συνετρίβησαν) by him and fled."

(9) In 13:51, when the citadel fell, "the Jews entered it with praise and palm branches, and with harps and cymbals and stringed instruments, and with hymns and songs, because a great enemy had been crushed (συνετρίβη) and removed from Israel."

(10) The concluding poem of section two (14:4–15) records that in Simon's time "no one was left in the land to fight . . . and the kings were crushed (συνετρίβησαν)" (14:13).

Thus, repeatedly, the enemies of the Jews are "crushed," and, in the light of 3:18–19 and 3:22, we may understand that there is a thread of divine assistance running from victory to victory.[16] This finding tempers

[15] Most scholars believe that the text is corrupt at 9:15, since Azotus, being in the coastal plain, had no mountain nearby. A number of commentators mention an attractive solution proposed in 1778 by J. D. Michaelis. (See, e.g., Grimm, *Das erste Buch der Maccabäer*, 135.) Michaelis suggested that in 9:15 Azotus (Hebrew Ashdod [*ʾšdwd*]) is a corruption of the word *ʾšdwt*, meaning "slopes," and thus we should read "the slopes of the mountain" in place of "Mount Azotus."

[16] 1 Maccabees draws a contrast between righteous Jews and Gentiles concerning this matter. As I indicated above, the text often uses the passive form of the verb συντρίβω in relation to Jewish victories, signifying divine assistance and double causality. The Jewish appeal for divine help in 3:52–53 underscores this understanding: "Here the Gentiles are assembled against us to destroy us; you know what they plot against us. How will we be able to withstand them, if you do not help us?" (Cf. Jonathan's instruction to his forces at 9:45–46 ["Look! the battle is in front of us and behind us. . . . Cry out now to Heaven that you may be delivered from the hands of our enemies"] and his words to the Spartans: "We have the help that comes from Heaven for our aid, and so we were delivered from our enemies" [12:15].) Gentiles, however, are portrayed as fighting alone (e.g., Seron declares: "I will make war on Judas and his companions" [3:14]) and claim victory for themselves. For instance, at 10:52–53 Alexander Balas announces: "I have returned to my kingdom and have taken my seat on the throne of my ancestors, and established my rule–for I crushed (συνέτριψα) Demetrius and gained control of our country."

the opinion of some scholars that the hand of God is rarely, if ever, seen in 1 Maccabees.[17]

Before moving on, I should note that the theme of double causality plays a part in furthering the pro-Hasmonean advocacy as well. As we have just seen, repeatedly it is the Hasmoneans whom God assists. This matter is highlighted by the following. In chapter two above we saw that in 5:55–62 an episode occurs involving two men—Joseph and Azariah—who had been asked by Judas to govern in his absence, but who were also told not to engage in any battles (cf. 5:19). Nonetheless, they moved against some Gentile forces and were defeated. In 5:62 we are told that these two failed because "they did not belong to the family of those men *through whom deliverance was given to Israel.*" Put another way, there was no double causality associated with the actions taken by these men as there was with the deeds of the Hasmoneans.[18]

[17] We read in Schürer (*The History of the Jewish People*, 3.1.180), for example, that in 1 Maccabees "the [Hasmonean] successes . . . appear throughout as resulting from the military ability and political sagacity of the Maccabaean-Hasmonaean princes."

[18] We should observe how Joseph and Azariah fail to make an appeal for divine assistance before they encounter the enemy. Indeed, the narrative underscores that they are acting like Gentiles in this regard since their words are remarkably similar to those of Seron at 3:14.

3:14	5:57
καὶ εἶπε	καὶ εἶπαν
ποιήσω ἐμαυτῷ ὄνομα	ποιήσωμεν καὶ αὐτοὶ ἑαυτοῖς ὄνομα
καὶ δοξασθήσομαι	
ἐν τῇ βασιλείᾳ	
καὶ πολεμήσω	καὶ πορευθῶμεν πολεμῆσαι
τὸν Ἰούδαν	πρὸς τὰ ἔθνη τὰ κύκλῳ ἡμῶν
καὶ τοὺς σὺν αὐτῷ	
τοὺς ἐξουδενοῦντας	
τὸν λόγον τοῦ βασιλέως	
[Seron] said,	So [Joseph and Azariah] said,
"I will make a name for	"Let us also make a name for
myself	ourselves;
and win honor	
in the kingdom.	
I will make war	let us go and make war
on Judas	on the Gentiles around us."
and his companions,	
who scorn the king's	
command."	

The Liberation of the Temple and the Citadel

We have just seen that 1.E highlights some important themes in 1 Maccabees. It is appropriate to investigate whether the structures of sections one and two convey any additional thematic meanings. In this regard, the reader will recall that I set aside a pair of episodes at the outset of chapter four and indicated that I would return to them in the present chapter. The episodes concern the liberation of the temple and the liberation of the citadel. This episodic similarity brings to mind Martola's claim that, above all, 1 Maccabees is the story of the liberation of Jerusalem. Indeed, evidence may be gathered which suggests that the two liberation events do seem to be highlighted in sections one and two.

To begin with, in numbers 4 and 9 in the previous section the two liberation episodes are linked by similar occurrences of the word συντρίβω. In 4:36, since, as they say, "our enemies are crushed (συνετρίβησαν)," Judas and his brothers move to liberate the temple. In 13:51 the Jews, under Simon, enter the liberated citadel with celebration "because a great enemy had been crushed (συνετρίβη)."

In addition, an obvious datum is the fact that the temple is liberated in section one (4:36–59), while the citadel is liberated in section two (13:49–51).[19] This bifurcated pattern is supported by the distributions of the words that are used in reference to the temple and the citadel in sections one and two. In order to facilitate the following discussion, we should recognize that in 1 Maccabees one Greek word is used for the citadel (ἄκρα), but two different words are used for the temple (ἁγίασμα and ἅγιον). In addition, there are some occurrences of ἅγιον in 1 Maccabees that do not refer to the temple.[20] In the following, I will be restricting my attention to those occurrences where the word does refer to the temple.

Let us consider the following chart, which summarizes the number of occurrences by section of the word ἄκρα,[21] as well as of the two words ἁγίασμα[22] and ἅγιον (when this word refers to the temple).[23]

[19] According to the text, the first action taken by Judas, following the death of Antiochus IV at the conclusion of section one, is to besiege the citadel (cf. 6:19–20). This suggests that the citadel will be an important concern in section two.

[20] For instance, 1:63 refers to the "holy covenant" (διαθήκην ἁγίαν).

[21] Section one: 1:33; 3:45; 4:2, 41. Section two: 6:18, 26, 32; 9:52, 53; 10:6, 7, 9, 32; 11:20, 21, 41; 12:36; 13:21, 49, 50, 52; 14:7.

[22] Section one: 1:21, 36, 37 (bis), 39, 45, 46; 2:7; 3:45; 4:38; 5:1; 6:7. Section two: 6:26, 51.

[23] Section one: 2:12; 3:43, 51, 58, 59; 4:36, 41, 43, 48. Section two: 6:18, 54; 7:33, 42; 9:54;

	Section One	Section Two
citadel		
ἄκρα	4	18
temple		
ἁγίασμα	12	2
ἅγιον	9	13

The pattern that may be observed in the chart is striking. Counting the two words ἁγίασμα and ἅγιον together, the temple is referred to in section one twenty-one times, but only fifteen times in section two. Conversely, the word ἄκρα appears only four times in section one, yet eighteen times in section two. Thus, section one has a concentration on the temple, which is liberated in 1.C′, and section two repeatedly mentions the citadel, which is liberated in 2.A′.

Still, one could object that the pattern which we have just observed is not surprising. For instance, it is reasonable that after the temple has been liberated it is not mentioned as much. Let us therefore return to the episodes when the temple and the citadel are liberated (4:36–59 and 13:49–52), for, as we will see, it is through these episodes that the strongest and clearest marking out and tying together of the two liberations takes place.

We will begin by observing the similarity between 4:54 and 13:51.

> At the very season and on the very day that the Gentiles had profaned [the altar], it was dedicated with songs (ἐν ᾠδαῖς) and lutes and harps and cymbals (καὶ κινύραις καὶ κυμβάλοις). (4:54)

> On the twenty-third day of the second month, in the one hundred seventy-first year, the Jews entered [the citadel] with praise and palm branches, and with harps and cymbals (καὶ ἐν κινύραις καὶ ἐν κυμβάλοις) and stringed instruments, and with hymns and songs (ἐν ᾠδαῖς), because a great enemy had been crushed and removed from Israel. (13:51)

10:39 (bis), 42, 44; 13:3, 6; 14:15 (bis). G. Neuhaus ("Quellen im 1. Makkabäerbuch? Eine Entgegung auf die Analyse von K.-D. Schunk," *JSJ* 5 [1974] 171) also provides a list of occurrences in 1 Maccabees of the terms ἁγίασμα and ἅγιον. There are some differences between our lists: in regard to ἁγίασμα Neuhaus cites 1:43 (following Codex Alexandrinus) but not 1:39, and for ἅγιον he does not record 7:33.

These are the only usages of the terms ᾠδή and κύμβαλον in 1 Maccabees. The word κινύρα, however, does appear a third time in the book.

> Jerusalem was uninhabited like a wilderness; not one of her children went in or out. The sanctuary was trampled down, and aliens held the citadel; it was a lodging place for the Gentiles. Joy was taken from Jacob; the flute and the harp (κινύρα) ceased to play. (3:45)

There is a fascinating web of connections at work here. In 3:45 the temple is trampled and the citadel is occupied by foreigners. This situation is marked by a loss of joy, together with the cessation of the playing of flutes and harps. The playing of harps returns in the book, however, on two occasions: when the temple is liberated (4:54) and when the citadel is liberated (13:51). Each occasion of liberation is also associated with a return of joy to the Jews. In regard to the liberation of the temple, in 4:56 the Jews celebrate the dedication of the altar for eight days and we are informed that they "joyfully (μετ' εὐφροσύνης) offered burnt offerings," and 4:58 tells us that "there was great joy (εὐφροσύνη μεγάλη) among the people." Then, in 4:59, the Jews decide to celebrate the event with joy annually, which is similar to Simon's decree at 13:52 regarding the liberation of the citadel.

4:59	13:52
καὶ ἔστησεν Ἰούδας	καὶ ἔστησε
καὶ οἱ ἀδελφοὶ αὐτοῦ	
καὶ πᾶσα ἡ ἐκκλησία Ισραηλ	
ἵνα ἄγωνται αἱ ἡμέραι	
τοῦ ἐγκαινισμοῦ τοῦ	
θυσιαστηρίου ἐν τοῖς	
καιροῖς αὐτῶν ἐνιαυτὸν	
κατ' ἐνιαυτὸν	κατ' ἐνιαυτὸν
ἡμέρας ὀκτὼ ἀπὸ τῆς	τοῦ ἄγειν
πέμπτης καὶ εἰκάδος τοῦ	τὴν ἡμέραν ταύτην
μηνὸς Χασελευ	
μετ' εὐφροσύνης καὶ χαρᾶς	μετ' εὐφροσύνης
Then Judas	Simon decreed
and his brothers	

and all the assembly of	
Israel determined	
that every year	that every year
at that season the days	they should celebrate
of dedication of the altar	this day
should be observed with joy	with joy.
and gladness for eight	
days, beginning with the	
twenty-fifth day of the	
month of Chislev.	

Moving on, the word καθαρίζω ("to purify") appears in 1 Maccabees five times and all but one are in the liberation episodes. In 4:36 Judas and his brothers, noting that their enemies have been "crushed," decide to go up "to cleanse the sanctuary (καθαρίσαι τὰ ἅγια)." 4:41 tells us that "Judas detailed men to fight against those in the citadel until he had cleansed the sanctuary (καθαρίσῃ τὰ ἅγια)." According to 4:43 the Jews indeed "cleansed the sanctuary (ἐκαθάρισαν τὰ ἅγια)." In 13:50 Simon "cleansed the citadel (ἐκαθάρισε τὴν ἄκραν)." The fifth appearance of καθαρίζω occurs just prior to this act, in 13:47, when Simon expelled his enemies from their homes in Gazara and "cleansed (ἐκαθάρισε) the houses in which idols were located." Thus, this occurrence is in close proximity to the liberation of the citadel.

In addition to the items we have just observed, the only two occurrences of the word αἴνεσις ("praise") in 1 Maccabees are found in the two liberation episodes. In 13:51 Jews enter the citadel "with praise (μετὰ αἰνέσεως)." Earlier, in 4:56, they had celebrated the dedication of the altar, joyfully offered burnt offerings, and offered a sacrifice of "well-being and praise (αἰνέσεως)."

All in all, given the correspondences we have just surveyed, it is apparent that the liberation of the temple and the citadel is an important theme in 1 Maccabees. Martola writes: "That the deliverance of [the citadel] was regarded as being important emerges from the mention of the joy of the people (13,51) and from the decision to celebrate the deliverance annually [13:52]."[24] In the light of the evidence, not only is this true as well concerning the liberation of the temple (joy: 4:56, 58, 59; annual celebration: 4:59), but

[24] Martola, *Capture and Liberation*, 180.

we may also add to the notes of joy and annual celebration the singing and playing of musical instruments that took place during both events (4:54 and 13:51), the presence of praise in both instances (4:56 and 13:51), and the purification rituals that occurred on both occasions (4:36, 41, 43 and 13:50).

Since the liberation of the temple was accomplished under the leadership of Judas, and the liberation of the citadel by Simon, it is striking that while each of these brothers receives a eulogy in 1 Maccabees (3:1–9 and 14:4–15), Jonathan does not. In addition, we may observe that in Mattathias' testament (2:49–68) he mentions Judas (2:66) and Simon (2:65), but he does not mention Jonathan. A reasonable explanation for this situation is that, while Jonathan was a great leader, he was not a liberator in the sense that Judas (the liberator of the temple) and Simon (the liberator of the citadel) were.

Conclusion

In this chapter we have observed how the structuring of sections one and two of 1 Maccabees highlights some important themes. The central subsection of section one (1.E) establishes the importance of Judas and his brothers, and also presents the theological premise that God cooperated in their victories. Several lines of evidence suggest that the liberation of the temple in section one and the citadel in section two is an additional important theme.

The results obtained in this chapter are noteworthy because they confirm each of the competing scholarly claims concerning the major theme of 1 Maccabees. The traditional view is that the work is meant to glorify the Hasmonean dynasty.[25] According to Martola, however, this theme is only a veneer, and the primary purpose of the book–its main story–is to convey the account of the capture and liberation of Jerusalem.[26] As we have seen, both the pro-Hasmonean advocacy and the liberation motif are prominent themes in sections one and two. In addition, we have observed the operation of a third theme, which is the notion of double causality.

Since I have now fully explored the structure and meaning of sections one and two, I will turn, in the following chapter, to take up the issue of section three.

[25] Cf. n. 8 above.

[26] See Martola, *Capture and Liberation*, 279.

CHAPTER 7

Section Three (14:16–16:24)

It is obvious that section three falls outside the chiastic structuring of sections one and two. What are we to make of this situation? Previous generations of scholars felt that 1 Maccabees had originally appeared in a shorter form, and the most commonly accepted theory held that the first edition had stopped at 14:15.[1] This, of course, marks the end of the chiastic structuring that we have observed, as well as the conclusion of Martola's main story, and it is also the approximate point at which Josephus seems to have stopped using 1 Maccabees as a source.[2] The convergence of these items is provocative. Have we encountered in the preceding pages new evidence that 1 Maccabees was expanded at some point?[3]

[1] The following scholars are among those who supported the idea that 14:15 was the original ending of 1 Maccabees: J. Destinon, *Die Quellen des Flavius Josephus in der Jüd. Arch. Buch XII-XVII = Jüd. Krieg Buch I* (Keil: Lipsius and Tischer, 1882) 11; Kautsch, "Das erste Buch der Makkabäer," 29, 31; and J. Wellhausen, *Israelitische und jüdische Geschichte* (Berlin: W. de Gruyter, 1921) 257.

[2] See R. Marcus, *Josephus* (LCL; Cambridge, MA: Harvard University; 1943) 7.334 n. d.; L. Feldman, *Josephus and Modern Scholarship (1937-1980)* (New York: W. de Gruyter, 1984) 222–23; and Schürer, *The History of the Jewish People*, 1. 50.

[3] See n. 18 in chapter four above in which I point out how 14:4–15 echoes 1:2–4, thus suggesting a framing of 1:1–14:15. Also see n. 19 in the same chapter where I show that 14:15 is chiastic. Thus, the chiastic structuring of sections one and two ends with a chiasm, neatly suggesting a conclusion. Further, it is important to recognize that the problems which appear in 1 Maccabees 1 are corrected in the material preceding the poem. As we have seen, under Judas' leadership the Jews cleansed the temple and restored the religious cult (4:36–57), and Simon overthrew the citadel and brought independence to the Jews (13:34–40, 49–51). Therefore, one may argue that sections one and two present a coherent and self-contained account.

Some literary critics would suggest that this question is not germane to the present study. For these scholars, rhetorical-critical study and historical-critical study are completely different endeavors that should be kept apart.[4] Given such an understanding, questions relating to diachronic analysis, which is interested in the history of a text's composition, are simply not relevant to rhetorical criticism. Rather, rhetorical criticism is solely committed to synchronic analysis and thus only considers a text as it now stands, in its final form.[5]

P. Trible, however, wisely cautions against accepting too readily a separation between diachronic and synchronic pursuits:

> Full rhetorical reading includes conversation with [historical disciplines.] The reading evaluates the findings of these disciplines in the light of its own research and its own synchronic goal. Sometimes the rhetorical critic deems the findings suspicious or gratuitous. Other times the critic concludes that a particular text manifests a history. In those cases the critic ponders how that past affects the final form. The possibilities are several. . . . Decisions come text by text to meet the requirements of particularity. *In general, rhetorical analysis begins and ends with the final form of a text,*

[4] M. Kessler ("A Methodological Setting for Rhetorical Criticism," 13–14), for instance, stakes out such a position (emphasis added):

> And now . . . something may be said in favour of form criticism limiting its field of operation to the analysis and history of genres, as well as their setting. The present tendency to broaden its tasks can only lead to more confusion. . . . *Why not press into service an older useful term with a long tradition: rhetorical criticism, for an exclusively* structural (in the broader senses), *synchronic preoccupation of the text. In this manner, diachronics would be represented well by source criticism and/or traditio-historical criticism, synchronic method would be served by rhetorical criticism, and form criticism would pursue the typical Gunkelian concerns* with genres, genre elements, their present as well as historical setting, the sociological setting of literary units from the smallest genre element, to the genre, the pericope, tradition blocks, and perhaps even entire biblical books. . . . *In sum, rhetorical criticism deserves serious consideration as a label for the leading candidate for synchronic criticism.*

[5] On rhetorical criticism as a synchronic endeavor, see J. Muilenburg, "A Liturgy on the Triumphs of Yahweh," *Studia Biblica et Semitica* (ed. W. C. van Unnik and A. B. van der Woude; Wageningen, Netherlands: H. Veenman en Zonen, 1966) 250–51; I. M. Kikawada, "Some Proposals for the Definition of Rhetorical Criticism," *Semitics* 5 (1977) 69; B. S. Childs (*Introduction to the Old Testament as Scripture* [Philadelphia: Fortress, 1979] 74); and Exum, "Aspects of Symmetry," 25 n. 1.

though it is not limited to that form. Synchronic analysis allows for diachronic reflection.[6]

The outline of my discussion in the present chapter mirrors Trible's understanding. I will begin with a brief consideration of themes in section three. I will then take up historical-critical concerns. I will close with an investigation of the meaning of section three as it now stands. Thus, I will provide both synchronic analysis and diachronic reflection, and I will begin and end—both literally and figuratively—with the final form of 1 Maccabees.

Rhetorical Beginning

I turn first to describe the role in section three of the prominent themes of sections one and two that we explored in the previous chapter. This line of inquiry will allow us to observe, at least in a partial fashion, how section three relates to the earlier sections. As the reader will recall, the structure of sections one and two led me to identify three major themes: a pro-Hasmonean advocacy, double causality, and the liberation motif. It will facilitate matters somewhat to deal with these themes, as they pertain to section three, in reverse order.

(1) Since by the time we reach section three both the temple and the citadel have been liberated, we might expect little attention to be paid to either institution in the section. Indeed, the citadel is mentioned in but two of the ninety-nine verses of section three. First, 14:36 states that in Simon's day the Gentiles were put out of the country, including "those who had built themselves a citadel." It may be observed that this verse resonates with the liberation motif. Second, we learn in 15:28 that Antiochus VII sent one of his Friends to Simon to try to regain various sites that Simon held, including the citadel.

[6] Trible, *Rhetorical Criticism*, 94 (emphasis added). Cf. the position of J. T. Walsh ("Genesis 2:4b–3:24: A Synchronic Approach," *JBL* 96 [1977] 161 n. 1): "Diachronic and synchronic exegesis must not be opposed as rivals but coordinated as complements." See also R. Melugin, "Muilenburg, Form Criticism, and Theological Exegesis," *Encounter with the Text* (ed. M. J. Buss; Philadelphia: Fortress, 1979) 92–96. A recent attempt to integrate synchronic and diachronic concerns may be found in G. Hens-Piazza, *Of Methods, Monarchs, and Meanings: A Sociorhetorical Approach to Exegesis* (Studies in Old Testament Interpretation 3; Macon, GA: Mercer University, 1996).

The temple, however, is mentioned seven times in section three.[7] Each time, the word ἅγιον is used. 7 appearances of this word in the 99 verses of section three is a rate of appearance per verse of approximately 7%. For the sake of comparison, the rate of appearance of ἅγιον (in reference to the temple) per verse in sections one and two is roughly 3% (22 appearances in 825 verses).[8] Obviously, there is still a relatively strong interest in the temple in section three. This finding will be of importance when I return to my synchronic analysis below.

(2) Double causality appears in section three at 16:3, when Simon addresses two of his sons, John and Judas, and tells them to "go out and fight for our nation, and may the help that comes from Heaven be with you (ἐκ τοῦ οὐρανοῦ βοήθεια ἤτω μεθ' ὑμῶν)." This statement is similar to two earlier passages in 1 Maccabees. First, in 3:19 Judas proclaims that "strength comes from Heaven (ἐκ τοῦ οὐρανοῦ ἰσχύς)." Second, in 12:15, in a letter that he has written to the Spartans, Jonathan states: "We have the help which comes from Heaven as our aid (ἔχομεν γὰρ τὴν ἐξ οὐρανοῦ βοήθειαν βοηθοῦσαν ἡμῖν)." Thus, each of the three brothers—Judas, Jonathan, and Simon—declares that God provides succor, and they use similar language to do so.[9]

(3) We come now to the pro-Hasmonean advocacy. An obvious illustration of the theme in section three comes at the conclusion, which, as we have already seen, seems to correlate John Hyrcanus with Judas. The reader will recall that 16:23–24 relates how "the rest of the acts of John and his wars and the brave deeds that he did" may be found in the annals of his high priesthood. This material is reminiscent of 9:22, which refers to "the rest of the acts of Judas, and his wars and the brave deeds that he did." While we observed in chapter three above that the language used in these two verses is mirrored elsewhere in 1 Maccabees (cf. 8:2 and 10:15), the linkage of John and Judas here is intriguing in the light of some further evidence.

In 16:4 John leads an army out to face Cendebeus.[10] They camp for the

[7] 14:29, 31, 36, 42, 43, 48; 15:7.

[8] For references, see n. 23 in chapter six above.

[9] Dancy (*A Commentary on I Maccabees*, 2 n. 1) suggests that the phrase "The Help of God" or "The Help of Heaven" may have been a watchword of the Hasmoneans, since a variant appears not only in these three places but also in 2 Macc 12:11.

[10] The Greek text of 16:4 does not name the figure who leads the forces: καὶ ἐπέλεξεν ἐκ τῆς χώρας εἴκοσι χιλιάδας ἀνδρῶν πολεμιστῶν καὶ ἱππεῖς, καὶ ἐπορεύθησαν ἐπὶ τὸν Κενδεβαῖον καὶ ἐκοιμήθησαν ἐν Μωδεϊν. Oesterley ("The First Book of Maccabees," 122),

night, and then, in 16:5, they march into a plain, opposite Cendebeus and his forces with a stream running between them. In 16:6 John sees that his soldiers are afraid to cross the stream, so he crosses first, and then they follow him. The Jews go on to victory and burn some towers in Azotus, where some of Cendebeus' troops had attempted to hide (16:7–10). This material is similar to 5:37–44, wherein Judas leads his troops across a stream. It will be useful for the present discussion, as well as for later analysis, to observe these passages together.

> After these things Timothy gathered another army and encamped opposite Raphon, *on the other side of the stream* (ἐκ πέραν τοῦ χειμάρρου). Judas sent men to spy out the camp, and they reported to him, "All the Gentiles around us have gathered to him; it is a very large force. They also have hired Arabs to help them, and they are encamped *across the stream* (πέραν τοῦ χειμάρρου), ready to come and fight against you." And Judas went to meet them. Now as Judas and his army drew near to *the stream of water* (τὸν χειμάρρουν τοῦ ὕδατος), Timothy said to the officers of his forces, "If he crosses over to us first, we will not be able to resist him, for he will surely defeat us. But if he shows fear and camps on the other side of the river, we will cross over to him and defeat him." When Judas approached *the stream of water* (τὸν χειμάρρουν τοῦ ὕδατος), he stationed the officers of the army at *the stream* (τοῦ χειμάρρου) and gave them this command, "Permit no one to encamp, but make them all enter the battle." Then *he crossed over against them first, and the whole army followed him* (διεπέρασεν ἐπ' αὐτοὺς πρότερος καὶ πᾶς ὁ λαὸς ὄπισθεν αὐτοῦ). All the Gentiles were defeated before him, and they threw away their arms and *fled* (ἔφυγον) into the sacred precincts at Carnaim. But he took the town and *burned the sacred precincts with fire* (τὸ τέμενος ἐνεπύρισαν ἐν πυρὶ), together with all who were in them. (5:37–44)

Goldstein (*I Maccabees*, 520), and Martola (*Capture and Liberation*, 184–85) believe that the leader of the forces is Simon himself. The majority of commentators, however, hold that the leader is John (see Grimm, *Das erste Buch der Makkabäer*, 231; Keil, "Commentar über die Bücher der Makkabäer," 249–50; Abel, *Les Livres des Maccabeés*, 278–79; Tedesche and Zeitlin, *The First Book of Maccabees*, 240; Dancy, *A Commentary on I Maccabees*, 192; Nelis, *1 Maccabeeën*, 252–53; and Doran, *The First Book of Maccabees*, 174). I side with this latter view. First, we are told in 13:53 that Simon appointed John to be the "commander of all the forces." Second, in 16:1–3, when John reports to Simon what Cendebeus has done, Simon addresses John and his brother Judas, telling them that he has grown old and that they should therefore take his place to "go out and fight for our nation." This statement immediately precedes 16:4.

> So John chose out of the country twenty thousand warriors and cavalry, and they marched against Cendebeus and camped for the night in Modein. Early in the morning they started out and marched into the plain, where a large force of infantry and cavalry was coming to meet them; and *a stream lay between them* (χειμάρρους ἦν ἀνὰ μέσον αὐτῶν). Then he and his army lined up against them. He saw that the soldiers were afraid to cross *the stream* (τὸν χειμάρρουν), so *he crossed over first; and when his troops saw him, they crossed over after him* (διεπέρασε πρῶτος, καὶ εἶδον αὐτὸν οἱ ἄνδρες καὶ διεπέρασαν κατόπισθεν αὐτοῦ). Then he divided the army and placed the cavalry in the center of the infantry, for the cavalry of the enemy were very numerous. They sounded the trumpets, and Cendebeus and his army were put to flight; many of them fell wounded and the rest *fled* (ἔφυγον) into the stronghold . . . but John pursued them until Cendebeus reached Kedron, which he had built. They also *fled* (ἔφυγον) into the towers that were in the fields of Azotus, and John *burned it with fire* (ἐνεπύρισεν αὐτὴν ἐν πυρί), and about two thousand of them fell. . . . (16:4–10)

Obviously, we may observe similar stories in these passages: the enemy of the Jews is on the other side of a stream; the Jewish leader crosses the water first, and his army follows him; the enemy forces are routed and flee, but the Jews burn them in their hiding places. The great similarity between the stories suggests a strong tie between John and Judas.

Diachronic Reflections

I turn now to a discussion of diachronic concerns. The fundamental issue is whether 1 Maccabees originally appeared in a form that was shorter than our present book. As I mentioned earlier, this is not a new hypothesis. The possibility of an original, shorter version of 1 Maccabees was raised during the first part of the nineteenth century, and J. Destinon provided the classic formulation of the theory in 1882.[11] In the wake of his work, several leading scholars accepted some form of the theory, including such prominent figures as E. Kautsch, G. Hölscher, and J. Wellhausen, and it became the majority opinion for several decades.[12] The most prevalent view among those who

[11] Destinon, *Die Quellen des Flavius Josephus*, 82, 85–86.

[12] See Kautzsch, "Das erste Buch der Makkabäer," 1. 30; G. Hölscher, *Die Quellen des Josephus für die Zeit vom Exil bis zum jüdischen Kriege* (Leipzig: Teubner, 1904) 9–10; and Wellhausen, *Israelitische und jüdische Geschichte*, 257 n. 1.

accepted the position was that 1 Maccabees had originally ended at 14:15 and 14:16–16:24 had been added by a later author or redactor; hence, the position became known as the "Addendum theory." Those who supported the Addendum theory depended primarily on the fact that Josephus, in his presentation of Jewish history in *Antiquities*, follows 1 Maccabees closely up through 1 Maccabees 13, but seems to quit using the book at approximately that point.

H. W. Ettelson, however, published in 1925 a thoroughgoing treatment of the issue in which he rejected the Addendum theory. Ettelson's major objection to the theory is that the evidence of Josephus constitutes an argument from silence. Ettelson also makes three claims in support of the overall unity of 1 Maccabees: (1) there is a uniform structure to the book; (2) there are similar literary and religious characteristics throughout the book; and (3) the book appears to have had a single translator. Following the publication of Ettelson's treatise the Addendum theory rapidly declined, and clearly the general consensus at present is that 14:16–16:24 has always been an integral part of 1 Maccabees.

Nonetheless, given the results of the present study, I believe that a fresh look at Ettelson's argumentation is warranted. I will begin by briefly surveying Ettelson's key points, after which I will critique his views. Let us turn first to Ettelson's claim that 1 Maccabees has a uniform structure. Ettelson writes:

> There is nothing on *a priori* grounds . . . either unnatural or inartistic for a history of the Maccabean struggle to have as its scope just what the present sixteen chapters of [1 Maccabees] cover. Herein is set forth the story of the Jewish Revolt . . . begun under Mattathias and carried through by his sons. The reign of Simon marked the triumph of the movement, and his death as the last representative of the generation of protagonists logically forms the close of the first period. It is indeed safe to assert that no one would have thought of questioning this on its own grounds as the rightful conclusion. The whole issue in fact has arisen only because of Josephus' apparent non-use of the last three chapters.[13]

Ettelson admits that stylistically 14:4–15 could be a conclusion, for the passage presents a glowing summary of Simon's career. Nevertheless, he disavows this notion and asserts that 14:4–15 is not meant to provide a conclusion, but rather what he calls a eulogistic summary by anticipation, which he holds is akin to the introductory encomium regarding Judas in

[13] Ettelson, "The Integrity of I Maccabees," 292.

3:1–9. Therefore, Ettelson concludes that 16:23–24 is the natural end of the book.

Ettelson also provides a disposition of 1 Maccabees. In his view, there is a general introduction, which ends with 2:70, that provides the causes of the revolt and describes the initial stages of the rebellion led by Mattathias. The rest of the book falls into two parts: (1) the struggle under Judas ending with his death at 9:22; and (2) the final stage of the struggle under the leadership of Jonathan and Simon, which ends at 16:24.[14]

As to Ettelson's claim that 1 Maccabees displays a unity in characteristics, his assertion is that there is a similar "feel" throughout 1 Maccabees. This impression derives from book-long similarities in general spirit and attitude, individual features, and literary manner and method. A few of Ettelson's examples of these similarities will suffice. First, he notes that the avoidance of the use of the word for Lord or God in 1 Maccabees is unique among the books of the LXX, and is present both in the early chapters and in the final ones. For instance, the phrase "by the divine mercy (ἐν τῷ ἐλέει)" in 16:3 recalls "by his mercy (ἐν τῷ ἐλέει αὐτοῦ)" in 2:57. Second, Ettelson discusses the way the genealogy of the Hasmonean family is handled in 1 Maccabees. In 2:1 we encounter a genealogy of Mattathias and his sons. It is noteworthy that they are not identified as Hasmoneans. Josephus, on the other hand, adds such an identification to the genealogy he provides in *Antiquities*. In keeping with 2:1, however, the genealogy given in 14:29 also leaves out the Hasmonean identification. Lastly, an example of a similarity of literary manner and method is the repetitiveness of the battle descriptions found throughout 1 Maccabees. This repetitiveness includes the formula "to sound the trumpets (σαλπίζω ταῖς σάλπιγξι)," which occurs eight times in 1 Maccabees, including 16:8 of the hypothetical Addendum.

Finally, Ettelson puts the importance of the matter of the unity of translation thus:

> If it is found that the last three chapters of [1 Maccabees] in the Greek not only are, like the first thirteen, a translation from the Hebrew, but what is more, that the translation in both instances is the work of one and the same hand, then it is obvious that these last three chapters, even were they an "Addendum," must have been incorporated as part and parcel of [1 Maccabees] before the book was translated into Greek. And if it is further found

[14] It may be seen that Martola's disposition of 1 Maccabees, which was presented in chapter one above, is in keeping with Ettelson's view.

> that Josephus used not the Hebrew original of [1 Maccabees] but the Greek translation thereof, then since this Greek translation as a version included from its very inception the whole sixteen chapters of our book, it follows that there could not have been a first edition in Greek of thirteen chapters circulating as an independent work complete in itself and as such constituting Josephus' source-book, which is what the Addendum theory presupposes.[15]

Ettelson subsequently marshals evidence intended to show: (1) that 1 Maccabees (including the last three chapters) is a translation from Hebrew; (2) that the translator of the final three chapters is the same person who translated the first thirteen chapters; and (3) that Josephus used the Greek version of 1 Maccabees exclusively.

Turning now to an evaluation of Ettelson's claims, it should be apparent that I reject his suggestions concerning the overall structure of 1 Maccabees. While we have observed the similarity between 9:22 and 16:23–24, this correspondence pales before the number of associations that support a division of 1 Maccabees into three sections, ending at 6:17, 14:15, and 16:24. We have reviewed these matters thoroughly above, especially in chapter five. I will also remind the reader that 9:1–57 is a connected passage that cuts across the putative boundary 9:22. In addition, it is difficult to understand how 14:4–15 can be a eulogistic summary by anticipation of Simon's career, as Ettelson would have it, by analogy to the introductory encomium of Judas at 3:1–9. For while 3:1–9 does precede Judas' career, 14:4–15 does not precede Simon's career. Simon becomes the leader of the Hasmonean cause at 13:8–9 in 143 BCE. The action of 13:49–52 occurs in 141. Thus, Simon is leader for at least two years before the supposed summary by anticipation is presented. Further, it is clear that 14:4–15 alludes to some events which take place earlier in the book. 14:7 relates that Simon "ruled over Gazara and Beth-zur and the citadel and he removed its uncleanness from it." As we have seen, Simon cleanses the citadel at 13:50. Moreover, he takes Gazara in 13:43–48 and Beth-zur in 11:65–66. Thus, the supposed anticipatory poem actually refers to some events that have already taken place in the text.

As to the matter of the presumed unity of translation of 1 Maccabees claimed by Ettelson, I agree with the overall point: based on Ettelson's evidence, there seems to have been one translator for the entirety of the book. Still, Ettelson's use of this finding to challenge the Addendum theory unrav-

[15] Ettelson, "The Integrity of I Maccabees," 307.

els through his insistence that Josephus knew only the Greek version of 1 Maccabees, since several scholars have claimed that he made some use of a Hebrew version as well.[16] If Ettelson cannot show conclusively that Josephus only knew 1 Maccabees in Greek, then, by his own admission, the most he can say is that the last three chapters, "even were they an 'Addendum,' must have been incorporated as part and parcel of [1 Maccabees] before the book was translated into Greek." Obviously, this assertion does not bring down the Addendum theory.

This leaves Ettelson's claim that there are uniform characteristics in 1 Maccabees. In the previous section of the present chapter I showed that the major themes of sections one and two are reflected in section three. Thus, we can agree with Ettelson in large measure. There is, however, a further consideration that demands our attention now. Simply put, there is another feature in sections one and two—namely, an anti-Gentile hostility—that does not recur in section three. As we will see, this difference appears to be of importance for the question of the unity of 1 Maccabees.

S. Schwartz draws our attention to the fact that one of the more obvious features of 1 Maccabees is a pronounced hostility to Gentiles. In his view, the clearest programmatic expression of this attitude is an address made by Simon at 13:3–6. This passage culminates with Simon stating: "all the nations have gathered together out of hatred to destroy us" (13:6).

A key facet of the anti-Gentile hostility in 1 Maccabees is, as Schwartz notes, the depiction of local Gentiles as thoroughly opposed to Jews. According to Schwartz:

> Though it is primarily the Seleucid armies who fight Israel, the author mentions the participation of locals whenever possible. Of the recruitment of troops for the first Seleucid campaign against Judas, [the author] writes (3:10): "And Apollonios gathered nations and from Samaria a great force to war against Israel." For the author's purposes and for ours, the question of the identity of the Samaritans—were they Samaritan hellenizers, as Abel (and perhaps Dancy) thought, or Macedonian colonists of the city of

[16] See especially M. Schwabe and E. Melamed, "Zum Text der Seronepisode in I Macc. und bei Josephus," *MGWJ* 72 (1928) 202–4; E. Z. Melamed, "Josephus and I Maccabees: A Comparison," *ErIsr* 1 (1951) 122–30 (in Hebrew); and Goldstein, *I Maccabees*, 14, 211, 247, 255, 294–95. For additional bibliography on this matter, see L. Feldman, "Josephus' Portrayal of the Hasmoneans Compared with 1 Maccabees," *Josephus and the History of the Greco-Roman Period* (ed. F. Parente and J. Sievers; Leiden: Brill, 1994) 41–42 n. 3.

Samaria, as Goldstein thinks, or some combination?—hardly matters. What is important, though, is that the author is *expressly* implicating the non-Judaean locals in the attack when he could have remained silent about the ethnic composition of the Seleucid force. Similarly, after Judas defeated Apollonios (3:25–27),

> The fear of Judas and his brothers, and fright, fell upon *the nations roundabout*. And his name reached as far as the king, and every nation (or, the whole nation) told of his campaigns. But when Antiochus heard these words (i.e., things) he was enraged and sent and gathered all the forces of his kingdom . . . (3:41) and there was joined to them a *force from Idumaea and the land of the foreigners* (i.e., Philistines . . .).[17]

Schwartz provides further examples of anti-Gentile hostility in 1 Maccabees, including some that mention local Gentiles, but we may judge the importance of the feature by the fact that some of the passages in the quote above involve material in 1.E, the central subsection in the chiastic structure of section one.

Given the evidence, Schwartz takes issue with the common dating of 1 Maccabees to ca. 100 BCE. He points out how at that time the Hasmoneans were in the midst of an expansion into neighboring lands and most of the local Gentiles were becoming judaized in some fashion. In this light, Schwartz writes:

> If the common dating of [1 Maccabees] to *c.* 100 B.C.E. is correct, we have before us an odd spectacle. [1 Maccabees] unquestionably promotes the Hasmonean dynasty, yet expresses hostility precisely to the nations now being patronized by them, and ambivalence about much of the dynasty's official manner of self-presentation; one would never guess that [1 Maccabees] was written in or near the court of John Hyrcanus I, a petty late Hellenistic monarch who gave all his sons Macedonian dynastic names and was protected by foreign mercenaries, or that of Aristobulus I, who actually styled himself "philhellene" (AJ 13.318); a court, furthermore, likely to have been full of Judaeans from all sorts of backgrounds, including hellenizing, and non-Judaean Jews who had been brought up as pagans and were still just barely Jewish. How can we account for this anomaly?[18]

Schwartz's solution is to propose a date of ca. 130 for the book, before the Hasmonean expansion. In order to assert this claim Schwartz suggests that

[17] Schwartz, "Israel and the Nations Roundabout," 24 (author's own emphasis).
[18] Schwartz, "Israel and the Nations Roundabout," 33.

16:23–24 may have been added at some point, since these verses imply that the reign of John Hyrcanus (d. 104) had ended.

What we must now observe is that the anti-Gentile hostility to which Schwartz points is present only in sections one and two of 1 Maccabees and is missing from section three. To underscore this point, let us review the primary material in section three that involves Gentiles in relation to Jews.

(1) Section three begins with positive portrayals of Gentiles. We are told in 14:16 that both the Romans and the Spartans were "deeply grieved" when they heard about the death of Jonathan. We are also informed in 14:17–23 and 15:15–24 that each nation renewed its friendship with the Jews.

(2) In the popular decree in honor of Simon we read of "Israel's enemies (τοὺς ἐχθροὺς Ισραηλ)" (14:26) and of "their enemies (οἱ ἐχθροὶ αὐτῶν)" (14:31). It should be noted that the identity of the enemies is not spelled out in these descriptions. To be sure, 14:36 does tell us that in Simon's day "the Gentiles (τὰ ἔθνη) were put out of the country." Yet, as Schwartz points out, "the reference is to the occupants of the fortresses" and the decree "nowhere congratulates the brothers for attacking gentiles."[19]

(3) 15:1–16:10 describes Jewish relations with Antiochus VII and his two agents, Athenobius and Cendebeus. At first, Antiochus, intending to lay claim to the throne and needing support from the Jews, offers various tax remissions and other favors, and tells Simon: "When we gain control of our kingdom, we will bestow great honor on you and your nation and the temple, so that your glory will become manifest in all the earth" (15:9). Antiochus later retracts his offers, however, and sends Athenobius to confer with Simon. Athenobius is to demand that Simon hand over certain cities or, in lieu thereof, to pay Antiochus a total of one thousand talents. Failing either move on Simon's part, Antiochus promises to "come and make war on you" (15:31). Athenobius visits Simon and delivers Antiochus' message, but Simon refuses to hand over the cities. He tells Athenobius that the Jews have merely recovered their own inheritance, "which at one time [was] unjustly taken by our enemies (ἐχθρῶν ἡμῶν)," and offers to pay only one hundred talents (15:33–35). In 15:36 Athenobius returns "in wrath" to Antiochus and reports to the king, and Antiochus becomes "very angry." He then instructs Cendebeus to subdue the Jews. Cendebeus invades Judea, but he is ultimately defeated.

In this material we see Gentiles being angry with the Jews, threatening

[19] Schwartz, "Israel and the Nations Roundabout," 30 n. 53.

them, and moving against them militarily. Yet investigation reveals that the descriptions of these matters are muted in comparison to earlier presentations in sections one and two. To be specific, there are three items in 15:1–16:10 that hearken back to passages in the earlier sections, but when they are presented in section three the element of anti-Gentile hostility which is present in the earlier passages disappears.

First, in 15:38–39 Antiochus VII splits his forces in two, giving one part to Cendebeus, while he takes the other with him to confront Trypho. This description is reminiscent of 3:34–37 wherein Antiochus IV takes half of his troops with him to the east, but leaves the other half to be led by Lysias against the Jews. In each case, the king also commissions his general.

> [Antiochus IV] turned over to Lysias half of his forces and the elephants, and gave him orders about all that he wanted done. As for the residents of Judea and Jerusalem, Lysias was to send a force against them to wipe out and destroy the strength of Israel and the remnant of Jerusalem; he was to banish the memory of them from the place, settle aliens in all their territory, and distribute their land by lot. (3:34–36)

> [Antiochus VII] made Cendebeus commander-in-chief of the coastal country, and gave him troops of infantry and cavalry. He commanded him to encamp against Judea, to build up Kedron and fortify its gates, and to make war on the people. (15:38–39)

As may be seen, the instructions given in these verses are markedly different. In 3:34–36 Antiochus IV intends for the Jews of Judea to be utterly wiped out, while in 15:38–39 Antiochus VII merely desires that they be defeated.

Second, in 16:2–3 Simon addresses two of his sons concerning the threat from Cendebeus and, as we will see, the address is similar to an earlier statement made by Simon.

> And Simon called in his two eldest sons Judas and John, and said to them: "I and my brothers and my father's house (ἐγὼ καὶ οἱ ἀδελφοί μου καὶ ὁ οἶκος τοῦ πατρός μου) have fought the wars of Israel from our youth until this day, and things have prospered in our hands so that we have delivered Israel many times. But now I have grown old, and you by Heaven's mercy are mature in years. Take my place and my brother's, and go out and fight for our nation, and may the help that comes from Heaven be with you." (16:2–3)

The wording ἐγὼ καὶ οἱ ἀδελφοί μου καὶ ὁ οἶκος τοῦ πατρός μου is arresting. It also appears in 13:3, when Simon speaks to the Jewish people in Jerusalem.

> You yourselves know what great things I and my brothers and my father's house (ἐγὼ καὶ οἱ ἀδελφοί μου καὶ ὁ οἶκος τοῦ πατρός μου) have done for the laws and the sanctuary; you know also the wars and the difficulties that my brothers and I have seen. By reason of this all my brothers have perished for the sake of Israel, and I alone am left. And now, far be it from me to spare my life in any time of distress, for I am not better than my brothers. But I will avenge my nation and the sanctuary and your wives and children, for all the nations have gathered together out of hatred to destroy us. (13:3–6)

The reader may observe the overall similarity between these two passages. Yet while 13:3–6 gives us anti-Gentile rhetoric ("all the nations have gathered together out of hatred to destroy us"[20]), 16:2–3 does not.

Third, we saw earlier that section three seems to connect John Hyrcanus and Judas through the presentation of an episode wherein John crosses a stream (16:4–10), which is similar to an earlier event when Judas does likewise (5:37–44). What I wish to point out now is that the earlier material features anti-Gentile hostility, but the material involving John—from section three—does not. The relevant passages were provided above. A review of this material will show that Gentiles are mentioned in 5:38, when Judas sends out spies who report back to him that "all the Gentiles around us (πάντα τὰ ἔθνη τὰ κύκλῳ ἡμῶν) have gathered to [Timothy]; it is a very large force (δύναμις πολλὴ σφόδρα)." We may further note that in this verse there is a reference to the Gentiles having "hired Arabs to help them." Conversely, in the material involving John, it simply states in 16:4 that he "marched against Cendebeus" and in 16:5 that "a large force (δύναμις πολλὴ)" of infantry and cavalry met him, but their ethnicity is not mentioned. Indeed, a comparison of 5:43 with 16:8 is revealing.

> Then [Judas] crossed over against them first, and the whole army followed him. The Gentiles (τὰ ἔθνη) were defeated before him, and they threw away their arms and fled into the sacred precincts at Carnaim. (5:43)

> They sounded the trumpets, and Cendebeus and his army were put to flight; many of them fell wounded and the rest fled into the stronghold. (16:8)

[20] Cf. 12:53, which concerns the Jews' situation following the death of Jonathan: "All the nations around them tried to destroy them, for they said, 'They have no leader or helper. Now therefore let us make war on them and blot out the memory of them from humankind.'"

As may be seen, these verses are roughly parallel. In each case, Jews are victorious and survivors among the enemy flee. Yet while in 5:43 we read about "the Gentiles (τὰ ἔθνη)" being defeated, 16:8 refers only to "Cendebeus and his army."

In sum, while section three reports about certain conflicts between the Jews on the one side, and Antiochus VII and his agents on the other, it does so with no evident hostility toward Gentiles. Thus, though Schwartz holds that 1 Maccabees reflects a stance of hatred toward Gentiles, this may fairly be said only of sections one and two of the book.

In the light of this finding, I suggest that if we take Schwartz's major point and combine it with the observations that I have made, we may derive the following theory. 1 Maccabees did appear in two editions. The first we may date to ca. 130. This edition was limited to sections one and two. It featured anti-Gentile hostility, because it appeared before the Hasmonean expansion. A second, longer edition—with section three appended—appeared ca. 100. This edition did not employ anti-Gentile rhetoric in its added material, because the Hasmonean expansion was in high gear. The uniformity of section three with what precedes could be explained by postulating that either it was the original author who added the new material for the second edition, or else the material was added by one of the author's students or other associates.

Thus, in the end, a theory of two editions makes sense of the literary evidence in 1 Maccabees. It is noteworthy that I have made no appeal to the evidence of Josephus, the bedrock of the proponents of the Addendum theory. Nevertheless, the position that I have just outlined offers a possible explanation for Josephus having stopped using 1 Maccabees. Suppose that the theoretical first edition appeared only in Hebrew, while the second, expanded edition—our present book—was eventually translated into Greek. As I mentioned above, several scholars have argued that Josephus made some use of a Hebrew version of 1 Maccabees. If he did know both a Greek and a Hebrew version, there is no necessity to assume that they were of equal length. If his Hebrew copy was of the hypothetical first edition and ended at 14:15, Josephus may not have fully trusted his Greek copy when it continued past that point.[21]

[21] Scholars have suggested a number of alternative factors that may have led Josephus to abandon 1 Maccabees near 14:15. These include the following. (1) 1 Maccabees 14–16 was simply missing in his copy. See Dancy, *A Commentary on I Maccabees*, 9, 31. (2) He anticipated switching sources to Nicolaus of Damascus. See Feldman, *Josephus and Modern Schol-*

Further Rhetorical Considerations

It is time to return to my synchronic investigation, and to investigate further the meaning of section three. For whether this material is original to 1 Maccabees, or was added at some point, in the end we should grapple with the text as it now stands. I suggested in chapter four that we view section three as a single literary unit, since it is framed by an inclusio. This inclusio, it will be remembered, mentions that first Simon, and then his son John, became high priest. As we will now see, section three has much more to say about the priesthood.

Let us begin by observing the use of the primary words that relate to the priesthood in 1 Maccabees: ἀρχιερεύς ("high priest") and ἱερεύς ("priest"). The distribution of these words is provocative. The following chart records the number of occurrences of each term in sections one and two,[22] as well as in section three.[23]

	Sections One and Two	**Section Three**
ἀρχιερεύς	9	11
ἱερεύς	11	8
Total	20	19

We may observe in the chart that there are 39 appearances of these words in 1 Maccabees—20 in sections one and two, and 19 in section three. Section three contains 99 verses, while there are 924 verses in 1 Maccabees as a whole. Thus, section three constitutes about ten per cent of 1 Maccabees (10.7%). Given these data, we may see that approximately half of the usages of the main terms of priestly vocabulary in 1 Maccabees appear in close to 10% of the text. In a similar vein, we should recall that there is a strong interest in the temple in section three.

Section three is not interested in the priesthood as a vague concept. Rather, it appears that Simon's high priestly line is of great significance in the section.

arship, 223. (3) The chronology of the final parts of 1 Maccabees would not fit with the chronology adopted by Josephus. See Ettelson, "The Integrity of I Maccabees," 266–68, and Goldstein, *I Maccabees*, 475.

[22] ἀρχιερεύς (10:20, 32, 38, 69; 12:3, 6, 7; 13:36, 42); ἱερεύς (2:1; 3:51; 4:42; 5:67; 7:14, 33, 36; 10:42; 11:23; 12:6, 20).

[23] ἀρχιερεύς (14:17, 23, 27, 30, 35, 41; 15:17, 21, 24; 16:12, 24); ἱερεύς (14:20 [bis], 28; 14:41, 44, 47; 15:1, 2).

Four times, the phrase "Simon and his sons" appears, and these are the only times it occurs in 1 Maccabees. These appearances fall into two groups.

First, the phrase is used at 14:25 and 14:49. These verses bracket the popular decree. In 14:25 the people ask, "How shall we thank *Simon and his sons*?," and then the decree commences. After the decree is given, orders are issued to have copies of it inscribed on bronze tablets and placed in a conspicuous place in the sanctuary, "so that *Simon and his sons* might have them" (14:49).

The second occurrence of the phrase "Simon and his sons" appears at 16:13 and 16:16. In the first of these verses, Simon's son-in-law Ptolemy is intent on killing Simon and his sons: "[Ptolemy] determined to get control of the country, and made treacherous plans against *Simon and his sons*, to do away with them" (16:13). Ptolemy hosted a banquet for Simon and two of his sons–Mattathias and Judas. According to 16:16, when "*Simon and his sons* were drunk, Ptolemy and his men rose up, took their weapons, rushed in against Simon in the banquet hall and killed him and his two sons, as well as some of his servants." 16:19–20 tells us that Ptolemy sent troops to take possession of the temple and to do away with John too, but John is warned in 16:21, and in 16:22 he seizes the men who have come to kill him. As we know, 1 Maccabees then comes to a close by informing us that the rest of John's acts are written "in the annals of his high priesthood, from the time that he became high priest after his father."

Let us reflect on all this evidence. We have seen that section three is saturated with priestly vocabulary, including the term ἀρχιερεύς. Further, the inclusio that frames the section highlights first Simon and then John as high priest. The fact that we are told both before and after the popular decree that it is for Simon and his sons looms large. Within the decree, at 14:41, "the Jews and their priests [resolve] that Simon should be their leader and high priest forever (εἰς τὸν αἰῶνα), until a trustworthy prophet should arise." By indicating that the decree is to thank Simon *and his sons*, and that copies are to placed in the sanctuary for Simon *and his sons*, the text is telling us that the decision to make Simon high priest forever means that *his line* will hold the high priesthood forever. That is, the text makes 14:41 of the popular decree apply not just to Simon, but to his line as well.[24] Finally, we have just seen that

[24] The importance of this observation is that the decree itself is ambiguous about Simon's line. Cf. the following comments by Sievers (*The Hasmoneans*, 126–27), in reference to 14:41.

> "In perpetuity" (εἰς τὸν αἰῶνα) has been understood as a reference to the hereditary character of [Simon's] position, but the Greek says nothing of this and Abel [*Les Livres des Maccabeés*, 260] pointed out that it may be a hebraized rendering of the common

the book ends by telling us that, despite a severe threat, Simon did indeed begin a high priestly line, since his son John was able to follow him as high priest. Thus, there is no reason to think that 16:23–24 was added to the rest of section three. Indeed, this material is integral to the overall message of the section: Simon successfully began a legitimate high priestly line when his son John succeeded him.

Martola holds that 1 Maccabees "ends abruptly, and, from a literary point of view, in an unsatisfactory way."[25] I must disagree. In the light of my analysis, the ending is very satisfactory because it conveys the message that Simon's line was successfully established, capping a theme that has been highlighted throughout section three. I would also argue that the ending is not abrupt, but provides a dramatic effect. Ptolemy has tried to annihilate Simon's line. He has succeeded in killing Simon and two of his sons. But we know that a third son—John Hyrcanus—still lives. Ptolemy sends men to try to kill John, but they are thwarted. The pace moves quickly, which underscores the importance of the result that John survived. Bar-Efrat has written that the pace of time as perceived by a reader is influenced by several factors, with monotony slowing it down but interest and suspense speeding it up. He also suggests that when a narrative is dynamic and condensed the reader's attention is focused on what is being related, and an expectation is built up concerning what is to follow.[26] Everything in the last verses of 1 Maccabees pushes the hearer/reader to the ultimate point: John became high priest after his father. There is interest and suspense as Simon and his sons are murdered. What, the hearer/reader may wonder, will become of the remaining son, John?[27] Time is condensed and verbs pile up in 16:21–22 as the dynamic narrative proceeds in an urgent manner:

> hellenistic formula for granting an office or honor "for life" (διὰ βίου). In fact, εις τὸν αἰῶνα like its Hebrew equivalent לעולם is sometimes used in connection with a person's lifelong activity or condition. Thus it does not necessarily suggest the institution of a new dynasty, and, in fact, its failure to mention Simon's descendants suggests that Abel's conjecture may be right.

Concerning Siever's point that 1 Macc 14:41 does not mention Simon's descendants, we may contrast the verse with a passage such as Exod 29:5–9, in which Aaron's descendants are specifically mentioned when the priesthood is given to them perpetually.

[25] Martola, *Capture and Liberation*, 18.

[26] Bar-Efrat, *Narrative Art*, 160.

[27] This is not the first time that the book provides such a dramatic moment of suspense for the hearer/reader. For instance, in 12:50 Jonathan's followers (and the hearer/reader) believe that he has been killed, and in 12:52 they mourn his presumed death. Thus, 13:12 comes as a jolt: "Then Trypho left Ptolemais with a large army to invade the land of Judah, *and Jonathan was with him under guard*." Since Jonathan is surprisingly still alive, the hearer/reader becomes curious as to what will happen to him.

> But someone *ran ahead* and *reported* to John at Gazara that his father and brothers *had perished*, and that *he* (sc. Ptolemy) *has also sent* men *to kill* you also. When *he heard* this, *he was* greatly *shocked*; *he seized* the men *who came to destroy* him *and killed* them, for *he had found out* that *they were seeking to destroy* him.

Then, in 16:23–24, the book closes immediately upon making the point that John succeeded his father, Simon, underscoring the significance of the transition: "The rest of the acts of John and his wars and the brave deeds that he did, and the building of the walls that he completed, and his achievements, are written in the annals of his high priesthood, from the time that *he became high priest after his father*."

Conclusion

In this chapter I have shown how the final form of 1 Maccabees coheres and how section three fits thematically with sections one and two by carrying forward the major themes of the earlier sections. Yet I have also raised the possibility that section three was added at some point to a first edition of 1 Maccabees which ended with 14:15. We have seen that the section is framed by an inclusio, suggesting that it may have been added as a single unit. If this in fact occurred, we may infer that section three was probably added because of the political exigencies of John Hyrcanus and/or his son Alexander Janneus, each of whom faced internal revolt.[28] Indeed, according to Josephus and rabbinic literature, John was asked by a Pharisee to give up the office of high priest, and open rebellion against Alexander came when he was exercising his priestly office.[29] Possibly in the face of such troubles, section three establishes that the leadership of the Jews—and the position of high priest—was handed down from the generation of Judas, Jonathan, and Simon to another generation. Particularly interesting in this regard is the connection that section three makes between John and Judas. The implication would seem to be that John was a worthy successor to the generation of his father.

Whether it was added at some point, or belongs to the original form of 1 Maccabees, section three supplies an important clarification of material in sections one and two. Without section three, a hearer/reader of the earlier

[28] For discussions of the pertinent issues, with bibliographies, see Grabbe, *Judaism From Cyrus to Hadrian*, 1. 301–4, and Schürer, *The History of the Jewish People in the Age of Jesus Christ*, 1. 200–28.

[29] See Schürer, *The History of the Jewish People*, 1. 213–14, 222–23.

material in 1 Maccabees could have some questions concerning Hasmonean leadership following the liberation of the citadel. 5:62 states that the Hasmoneans were "the family . . . through whom deliverance was given to Israel." But what about after the deliverance (liberation)? Further, was a Hasmonean high priestly line legitimate? In 1 Maccabees 2 Mattathias is presented as a second Phinehas when he kills a Jew who is about to make a pagan sacrifice. The text is explicit about making the connection: "Thus [Mattathias] burned with zeal for the law, just as Phinehas did against Zimri son of Salu" (2:26).[30] In 2:54 Mattathias tells his sons: "Phinehas our ancestor, because he was deeply zealous, received the covenant of everlasting priesthood." Thus, with respect to both piety and genealogy Mattathias is rightful heir to the priestly line of Phinehas. Indeed, it is commonly held by scholars that this material about Phinehas supports the claim of the Hasmoneans to the high priesthood.[31] Yet nothing is said about Phinehas or any Hasmonean line in section two when Jonathan becomes high priest (10:20) and is twice reconfirmed in the position (11:27, 57). Confusion about the matter on the part of the hearer/reader is therefore a possibility. Section three, however, makes it clear that Simon was not a liberator only, but was also the legitimate post-liberation leader and progenitor of a high priestly line.

[30] Cf. Num 25:6–14.

[31] See, e.g., V. Aptowitzer, *Parteipolitik der Hasmonäerzeit im rabbinischen und pseudoepigraphischen Schrifttum* (New York: Kohut Foundation, 1927) 4–12.

CHAPTER 8

Concluding Observations

A convenient way to conclude this study is to compare the structure of 1 Maccabees that I have advanced with previous analyses. Through this process, I will be able to summarize my contribution.

The Standard Disposition

There is virtual unanimity among scholars that 1 Maccabees is to be divided along the following lines.

A. Introduction	1–2
B. Judas	3:1–9:22
C. Jonathan	9:23–12:53
D. Simon	13–16

The fundamental shortcoming in regard to this arrangement is that it is not based on a critical evaluation of the structure of the book. Instead, scholars appear to presume that this division is self-evident. Abel, for instance, merely announces, with no further discussion, that: "Le corps de l'ouvrage se divise ensuite en trois sections consacrées respectivement à Judas Maccabée, à Jonathan et à Simon."[1]

[1] Abel, *Les Livres des Maccabées*, xxx.

Martola's Dispositions

Martola's overall disposition of 1 Maccabees follows.[2]

I. Preparation	1–2
A. The emergence of the crisis, against the background of which the Hasmoneans appear as the deliverers of Israel	1
B. Matthathias turns to active resistance and entrusts his sons with continuing this task	2
II. The story of the first generation of the Hasmoneans	3–16
A. The achievements of Judas	3:1–9:22
B. The achievements of Jonathan and especially of Simon; the leadership passes to the next generation	9:23–16:24

In essence, the only thing Martola has changed here from the standard disposition is to contract units C and D of the standard disposition into his section II.B.[3]

Yet, this overall disposition is somewhat illusory, for the bulk of Martola's study is concerned with uncovering the "story within the story" of 1 Maccabees. As I explained in chapter one, Martola separates 1 Maccabees into its smallest components and then systematically links the majority of them–according to meaning and literary cohesion–into a coherent account, the main story. We will see below that he offers several alternative dispositions of the main story, but the following is his final disposition of it.[4]

[2] Martola, *Capture and Liberation*, 279.

[3] As we saw in the previous chapter, Ettelson also contracted units C and D of the standard disposition into a single unit.

[4] Martola, *Capture and Liberation*, 271.

Prologue 1:1–10

I. The origin of an imbalance	1:11–64
A. The apostasy of the people	1:11–15
B. The visitation as a consequence of the apostasy	1:16–64
II. The balance is restored	2–7; 9–11; 12:24–14:15
A. The zeal of Mattathias	2:1–70
B. The deflection of the visitation as a consequence of the zeal of Mattathias	3–7; 9–11; 12:24–14:15

Here we do see a major change from the standard disposition. Martola has discovered a story line that runs through most of 1 Maccabees: the origin of an imbalance caused by the occupation of the temple and the construction of the citadel, and the restoration of balance through liberation. To him, this story dominates the book: "It is . . . difficult to avoid becoming captured by the theme of the 'main story': capture and deliverance. That shows how powerful that theme is in [1 Maccabees] and . . . how thinly the theme of the whole of [1 Maccabees] is spread above that."[5] Given the dominance of the main story, Martola considers the whole of 1 Maccabees to be, simply, the main story plus some additions—8:1–32, 12:1–23, and 14:16–16:24.

Martola's work represents a step forward because he paid close attention to literary connections in 1 Maccabees (though he paid no systematic attention to the role of repetition in the book). As much of an advance as Martola's work is, however, his results are not entirely satisfying. In particular, one gets the impression that by having so much material lumped together in section II.B (3–7, 9–11, 12:24–14:15), there is an underlying imbalance to Martola's disposition of the main story.

The Disposition Given in the Present Study

We come, then, to my disposition of 1 Maccabees. We have observed that, by focusing on the role of repetition in the book, I have been able to isolate three main sections within it: section one (1:1–6:17); section two (6:18–

[5] Martola, *Capture and Liberation*, 279.

14:15); and section three (14:16–16:24). The first two sections emphasize the work of liberation of the temple and the citadel that was accomplished under Judas and Simon, promote a pro-Hasmonean advocacy, and assert double causality. Section three also touches on these themes, but stresses the establishment of Simon's high priestly line.

As we have seen, section three seems to consist of a single literary unit (14:16–16:24), but sections one and two are chiastic structures, each composed of several units. The following charts summarize these structures.[6]

Section One

A 1:1–10 Alexander the Great dies; Antiochus IV is introduced
 B 1:11–15 Renegade Jews seek to join with the Gentiles around them
  C 1:16–64 The temple is desecrated by the Greeks
   D 2:1–70 Mattathias urges his sons to rebel
    E 3:1–26 Judas leads the Jewish revolt
   D′ 3:27–4:35 Antiochus IV seeks to quell the Jewish revolt
  C′ 4:36–61 The temple is liberated and rededicated by the Jews
 B′ 5:1–68 Righteous Jews defeat the Gentiles around them
A′ 6:1–17 Antiochus IV dies

Section Two

A 6:18–7:50 The Jews obtain freedom of religion
 B 8:1–32 The Jews make a treaty with Rome
  C 9:1–10:66 Jonathan rises in power
  C′ 10:67–11:74 Jonathan maintains his powerful status
 B′ 12:1–23 The Jews renew their treaty with Rome
A′ 12:24–14:15 Simon liberates the citadel and obtains independence

[6] Butterworth (*Structure*, 60) observes that

> We must be aware of . . . the probability that several different rationales could be suggested for any particular unit [of a text]. There is a strong danger of reading our own structures into the text when we supply the headings or labels for the sections to be compared.

I agree in principle with this admonition, and have focused, throughout my investigation, on the actual wording of the important structural repetitions in 1 Maccabees. The headings, or summaries, in the following charts are meant solely to help the reader grasp the overall relationships among the various subsections in the chiastic structures in 1 Maccabees.

In certain respects, Martola and I offer similar arguments: his main story is akin to my sections one and two; we both hold that the theme of liberation is important in 1 Maccabees; and we entertain the possibility that 14:15 was the original ending of the book, with 14:16–16:24 being added at some point. This overall similarity is impressive, for we have employed different methodological approaches.

Nonetheless, it is clear that we have areas of disagreement.[7] For instance, Martola regards 8:1–32 and 12:1–23 as "islands" and additions, whereas in my disposition this material (2.BB′) plays an important structural role. Further, while Martola himself notes that 9:1–57 is a "rounded whole" which therefore crosses the putative boundary 9:22, he nevertheless maintains a boundary at that place in his overall disposition of 1 Maccabees. Conversely, I do not have a boundary at 9:22 in my disposition, where 9:1–57 is part of subsection 2.C. In addition, my analysis suggests that the pro-Hasmonean theme is not merely a veneer, as Martola maintains, but is instead a major component of the book.

I believe that my disposition offers two general advantages over Martola's. First, unlike Martola's section II.B of the main story, there is an obvious balance to the chiastic structuring that I have proposed for sections one and two. The material flows from subsection to subsection, and there are numerous formal symmetries between paired subsections.

Second, the structural patterning of sections one and two highlights important themes in the book. Section one contains an episode in which the Jews liberate and purify the temple (1.C′), which is emphasized by being pitted against a matching subsection (1.C) in which the temple is desecrated by the Greeks. The section ends with the death of Antiochus IV, the king who caused the imbalances that led to the work of liberation. Section two contains an episode in which the Jews liberate and purify the citadel (2.A′), and ends with the notice that Simon ruled over the citadel (14:7) and "made the sanctuary glorious" (14:15). The two liberation episodes are linked by repeated themes and wording. In addition, the role of the Hasmonean brothers, as well as the idea of double causality, are highlighted by the only central subsection in the two chiastic structures, 1.E. As we have seen, this subsection ends by observing that "Judas and his brothers began to be feared, and terror fell on the Gentiles all around them" (3:25), and at 3:19 Judas

[7] A vivid illustration of our differences is that, while I find a high degree of structure in 1 Maccabees, Martola (*Capture and Liberation*, 129) believes it is a "fact that [1 Maccabees] is rather loosely structured."

announces: "It is not on the size of the army that victory in battle depends, but strength comes from Heaven."

The importance of the structural highlighting of themes in my disposition may be underscored by the following. At one point in his study (and one should note that this is before he has decided to include 1 Maccabees 2 as part of the main story), Martola considers various ways to divide the main story (1 Macc 1; 3–7; 9–11; 12:24–14:15). He states that there are "at least three different criteria" by which one can do so:

> a) one which starts from the instances in which the balance is restored, at least the two main instances: 4,36–59 and 13,49–52; b) one which starts from the function of the verse 9,73 as a "watershed"; c) one which starts from the fact that 9,19–22 concludes a "history of Judas" within the block of text.[8]

Having outlined these possibilities, Martola turns to consider each in turn, and supplies a disposition to accompany each viewpoint. The disposition for the first viewpoint follows.

I	The attack against Jerusalem. Its background and origin	1 Macc 1
II	The work of liberation	1 Macc 3–7; 9–11; 12:24–14:15
	Poetic frame	3:3–9
	A. Main objective 1: The liberation from "the abomination of desolation" and the reintroduction of the "rightful" cult	3:10–4:61
	B. Main objective 2: The liberation from the control of Jerusalem by the heathens	5–7; 9–11; 12:24–14:3
	Poetic frame	14:4–15

[8] Martola, *Capture and Liberation*, 203. In regard to 9:73 being a "watershed," it is Martola's contention that after this point in 1 Maccabees the confrontation between the Jews and the Seleucids is no longer a religious threat. The charts which follow are derived, with slight alterations, from Martola, *Capture and Liberation*, 204–7.

According to Martola, the consideration of 9:73 as a "watershed" in 1 Maccabees leads to a division of the second part of the main story into two sections: (1) 3–7, 9; and (2) 10–11; 12:24–14:15. The most important difference between these two sections is that in the first the Torah-abiding Jews are opposed to the Seleucid powers, while in the second they are allied in some way with those in power. The disposition that Martola offers for this viewpoint follows.

I	The attack against Jerusalem. Its background and origin	1 Macc 1
II	The work of liberation	1 Macc 3–7; 9–11; 12:24–14:15
	Poetic frame	3:3–9
	A. The work of liberation is realized in direct conflict between Jerusalem and Antioch	3:10–7:50; 9
	B. The work of liberation is realized in indirect conflict between Jerusalem and Antioch	10–11; 12:24–14:3
	Poetic frame	14:4–15

In regard to the third possibility, Martola reminds us that the idea of 3:1–9:22 as a main section of 1 Maccabees is accepted almost without exception by scholars. He remarks that if one were to attach a heading to this material, such as "Judas as a leader for the work of liberation," one then has to decide whether to have separate following sections for Jonathan and Simon as well, or, as an alternative, to combine them into one section. Martola opts for the latter option. His disposition for the third viewpoint follows.

I	The attack against Jerusalem. Its background and origin	1 Macc 1
II	The work of liberation	1 Macc 3–7; 9–11; 12:24–14:15
	Poetic frame	3:3–9

A. The work of liberation is carried on under the leadership of Judas — 3:10–7:50; 9:1–22

B. The work of liberation is carried out under the leadership of Jonathan and Simon — 9:23–11:74; 12:24–14:3

Poetic frame — 14:4–15

Martola winds up rejecting the second possibility and its accompanying disposition. Instead of accepting either of the other possibilities outright, however, Martola thinks it best to combine them. This action is taken because in the first proposal the importance which Judas and his brothers undoubtedly have is not given due consideration, while in the third proposal the goals arrived at are not taken into account. In his proposed compromise Martola leans closer to the third proposed disposition, but he notes that "the heading is changed so that it appears that the [first] proposal is also of importance."[9] The resulting disposition follows.

I The attack against Jerusalem. Its background and origin — 1 Macc 1

II The work of liberation — 1 Macc 3–7; 9–11; 12:24–14:15

Poetic frame — 3:3–9

A. The work of liberation reaches its first main objective and continues under the leadership of Judas — 3:10–7:50; 9:1–22

B. The work of liberation continues and is brought to an end under the leadership of Jonathan and Simon — 9:23–11:74; 12:24–14:3

Poetic frame — 14:4–15

[9] Martola, *Capture and Liberation*, 207. Note the graphic illustration of the slipperiness of the use of headings or titles. Cf. n. 6 above.

Thus, at this point in his work Martola comes to the conclusion that the main story centers on the work of liberation and also involves the role of the brothers. Yet when he provides his final disposition for the main story—one that includes 1 Maccabees 2—these items (particularly the role of the brothers) are lost. This point may be verified by reviewing the disposition, which was supplied above. A strength of my disposition, then, is that, in contradistinction to Martola's final disposition of the main story, the thematic items that Martola himself singles out earlier in his study appear. As we have observed, my disposition highlights the liberation of the temple and the citadel as well as the role of the brothers.

Conclusion

In Butterworth's critique of various studies of structure he complains, in regard to one scholar, that no procedural rationale is provided; that only subjective criteria are used to decide which correspondences are significant with respect to structure; that all the data available are not considered; and that rival theories have not been evaluated.[10]

Throughout this investigation, I have tried to align my work with the general methodological approach that Butterworth suggests as a means of avoiding such drawbacks. In chapter one I clearly explained my procedural steps. In chapter two, beginning from the work of previous scholars, I isolated literary units in 1 Maccabees without considering the overall structure of the book. In chapter three I began to investigate whether instances of repetition might link any of these units and all cases that met certain criteria were taken into account. The resulting theory of the architecture of 1 Maccabees presented in chapter four was thus constructed on the basis of objectively identified evidence. In chapter five I obtained confirmation of the hypothetical tripartite structure of 1 Maccabees proposed in chapter four by investigating instances of formal symmetry between paired subsections of sections one and two. In chapter six I took up the question of the thematic highlighting performed by the chiastic structures of these sections. In chapter seven I examined section three from the standpoint of both diachronic and synchronic concerns. In the present chapter I have closed my investigation by evaluating alternative theories of the structure of 1 Maccabees.

[10] See chapter one above.

I noted at the outset of this study that scholars have focused on 1 Maccabees almost completely as a work of history.[11] While I agree that it is a valuable historical source, I hope to have demonstrated that 1 Maccabees gives us not simply history, but also literary art.[12] In the interests of a more full understanding of the book, it is time to begin reading this artistic work through new eyes.

[11] R. D. Nelson ("The Anatomy of the Book of Kings," *JSOT* 40 [1988] 39) makes an observation concerning 1–2 Kings that is applicable to 1 Maccabees as well: "we continue to read Kings automatically as history, a convention of reading we have set aside in approaching, let us say, Genesis or the Gospels." (Since Nelson wrote these words, however, several studies of literary artistry in 1–2 Kings have appeared. See Watson and Hauser, *Rhetorical Criticism of the Bible*, 59–61.)

[12] How underappreciated 1 Maccabees is as literary art can be gathered from a remark made by Goldstein (*I Maccabees*, 258), in which he compares 1 Macc 3:38–4:25 and 2 Macc 8:9–36. He writes (emphasis added):

> Both here [in 1 Maccabees] and in [2 Maccabees] the two commanders, Nicanor and Gorgias, are mentioned. Here, attention is focused on Gorgias; there, on Nicanor. The difference need not reflect a difference in sources but rather a difference in the author's interests. *Here, we can see the hand of the admirer of Hasmonean Judas,* who out-generaled the wily Gorgias. *There, we can see the hand of the literary artist*, who organized his narrative in parallel sections around the Feast of Dedication and the Day of Nicanor.

For a discussion of the structure of 2 Maccabees, see R. Doran, *Temple Propaganda: The Purpose and Character of 2 Maccabees* (CBQMS 12; Washington, DC: Catholic Biblical Association of America, 1981) 47–76.

Selected Bibliography

Abel, F.-M., *Géographie de la Palestine* (Paris: Gabalda, 1967).

——, *Les Livres des Maccabées* (Paris: Gabalda, 1949).

——, and J. Starcky, *Les Livres des Maccabées* (Paris: Cerf, 1961).

Alter, R., *The Art of Biblical Narrative* (New York: Basic Books, 1981).

Amit, Y., "Judges 4: Its Contents and Form," *JSOT* 39 (1987) 89–111.

——, "The Dual Causality Principle and its Effects on Biblical Literature," *VT* 37 (1987) 385–400.

Aptowitzer, V. *Parteipolitik der Hasmonäerzeit im rabbinischen und pseudoepigraphischen Schrifttum* (New York: Kohut Foundation, 1927).

Arenhoevel, D., *Die Theokratie nach dem 1. und 2. Makkabäer* (Mainz: Matthias Grünewald, 1967).

Arnold, P. M. "Mizpah." *ABD* 4. 879–81.

Art and Meaning: Rhetoric in Biblical Literature (ed. D. J. A. Clines et al.; JSOTSup 19; Sheffield: Sheffield Academic, 1982).

Bar-Efrat, S., *Narrative Art in the Bible* (JSOTSup 17; Sheffield: Almond, 1989).

——, "Some Observations on the Analysis of Structure in Biblical Narrative," *VT* 30 (1980) 154–73.

Bar-Kochva, B., *Judas Maccabaeus: The Jewish Struggle against the Seleucids* (Cambridge: Cambridge University, 1988).

Bartlett, J. R., *The First and Second Books of the Maccabees* (Cambridge: Cambridge University, 1973).

Berlin, A., *Poetics and Interpretation of Biblical Narrative* (Sheffield: Almond, 1983).

Bévenot, H., *Die Beiden Makkabäerbücher* (Bonn: Peter Hanstein, 1931).

Bickerman, E. J., *The God of the Maccabees: Studies on the Meaning and Origin of the Maccabean Revolt* (SJLA 32; Leiden: Brill, 1979).

———, *Institutions de Séleucides* (Paris: Geuthner, 1938).

Boda, M. J., "Chiasmus in Ubiquity: Symmetrical Mirages in Nehemiah 9," *JSOT* 71 (1996) 55–70.

Brettler, M., "The Structure of 1 Kings 1–11," *JSOT* 49 (1991) 87–97.

Bringmann, K., *Hellenistische Reform und Religionsverfolgung in Judäa: Eine Untersuchung zur jüdisch-hellenistische Geschichte (175–163 v. Chr.)* (Göttingen: Vandenhoeck & Ruprecht, 1983).

Butterworth, M., *Structure and the Book of Zechariah* (JSOTSup 130; Sheffield: Sheffield Academic, 1992).

Cardauns, B., "Juden und Spartaner," *Hermes* 95 (1967) 317–24.

Chiasmus in Antiquity: Structures, Analyses, Exegesis (ed. J. W. Welch; Hildesheim: Gerstenberg, 1981).

Clark, D. J., "Criteria for Identifying Chiasm," *Linguistica Biblica* 35 (1975) 63–72.

Collins, J. J., *Daniel, First Maccabees, Second Maccabees* (Wilmington: Michael Glazier, 1981).

Craven, T., *Artistry and Faith in the Book of Judith* (SBLDS 70; Chico, CA: Scholars, 1983).

Dancy, J. C., *A Commentary on I Maccabees* (Oxford: Basil Blackwell, 1954).

Destinon, J., *Die Quellen des Flavius Josephus in der Jüd. Arch. Buch XII–XVII = Jüd. Krieg Buch I* (Keil: Lipsius and Tischer, 1882).

Dillard, R. B., "The Literary Structure of the Chronicler's Solomon Narrative," *JSOT* 30 (1984) 85–93.

Dommershausen, W., *1 Makkabäer 2 Makkabäer* (Würzburg: Echter, 1985).

Donner, H., "Der Freund des Königs," *ZAW* 73 (1961) 269–77.

Doran, R., *The First Book of Maccabees: Introduction, Commentary, and Reflections* (New Interpreter's Bible 4; Nashville: Abingdon, 1996).

———, *Temple Propaganda: The Purpose and Character of 2 Maccabees* (CBQMS 12; Washington: Catholic Biblical Association, 1981).

Eskenazi, T. C., "The Structure of Ezra-Nehemiah and the Integrity of the Book," *JBL* 107 (1988) 641–56.

Ettelson, H. W., "The Integrity of I Maccabees," *Transactions of the Connecticut Academy of Arts and Sciences* 27 (1925) 249–384.

Exum, J. C., "Aspects of Symmetry and Balance in the Samson Saga," *JSOT* 19 (1981) 3–29.

——, "Promise and Fulfillment: Narrative Art in Judges 13," *JBL* 99 (1980) 43–59.

Feldman, L. H., *Josephus and Modern Scholarship (1937–1980)* (New York: de Gruyter, 1984).

——, "Josephus' Portrayal of the Hasmoneans Compared with 1 Maccabees," in *Josephus and the History of the Greco-Roman Period* (ed. F. Parente and J. Sievers; Leiden: Brill, 1994) 41–68.

Fischer, T., *Seleukiden und Makkabäer* (Bochum: Brockmeyer, 1980).

Fishbane, M., *Text and Texture* (New York: Schocken, 1979).

Frisch, A., "The Narrative of Solomon's Reign: A Rejoinder," *JSOT* 51 (1991) 22–24.

——, "Structure and Its Significance: The Narrative of Solomon's Reign (1 Kings 1–12.24)," *JSOT* 51 (1991) 3–14.

Gauger, J.-D., *Beiträge zur jüdischen Apologetik* (Cologne/Bonn: Hanstein, 1977).

Geiger, A., *Urschrift und Übersetzungen der Bibel* (2d ed.; Frankfurt/Main: Madda, 1928).

Gitay, Y., "Rhetorical Criticism," in *To Each Its Own Meaning: An Introduction to Biblical Criticisms and their Applications* (ed. S. L. McKenzie and S. R. Haynes; Louisville, KY: Westminster/John Knox, 1993) 135–49.

Goldstein, J. A., *I Maccabees* (AB 41; Garden City, N.Y.: Doubleday, 1976).

Grabbe, L. L., *Judaism from Cyrus to Hadrian* (Minneapolis: Fortress, 1992).

Grimm, C., *Das erste Buch der Maccabäer* (Leipzig: S. Hirzel, 1853).

Harrington, D., *The Maccabean Revolt: Anatomy of a Biblical Revolution* (Wilmington: Glazier, 1988).

Hauser, A. J., "Notes on History and Method," *Rhetorical Criticism of the Bible. A Comprehensive Bibliography with Notes on History and Method* (ed. D. F. Watson and A. J. Hauser; New York: Brill, 1994) 3–20.

Hearing and Speaking the Word: Selections from the Works of James Muilenburg (ed. T. F. Best; Chico, CA: Scholars, 1984).

Hölscher, G., *Die Quellen des Josephus für die Zeit vom Exil bis zum jüdischen Kriege* (Leipzig: Teubner, 1904).

Joüon, P., "Quelques hébraïsmes de syntaxe dans le premier livre des Maccabées," *Bib* 3 (1922) 204–6.

Kautzsch, E., "Das erste Buch der Makkabäer." *Die Apokryphen und Pseudepigraphen des Alten Testaments* (1900; reprint, Hildesheim: Georg Olms, 1962).

Keil, C., *Commentar über die Bücher der Makkabäer* (Leipzig: Dörffling und Francke, 1875).

Kikawada, I. M., "Some Proposals for the Definition of Rhetorical Criticism," *Semitics* 5 (1977) 67–91.

Lefèvre, A., "Maccabées (Livres I et II des.)," *DBSup* 5 (1957) 597–612.

Longman, T., *Literary Approaches to Biblical Interpretation* (Grand Rapids, MI: Zondervan, 1987).

Lundbom, J. R., "The Inclusio and Other Framing Devices in Deuteronomy I–XXVIII," *VT* 46 (1996) 296–315.

Maccabaeorum Liber I (ed. W. Kappler; Vetus Testamentum Graecum 9/1; Göttingen: Vandenhoeck & Ruprecht, 1936).

Mandell, S. R., "Did the Maccabees Believe that They Had a Valid Treaty with Rome?," *CBQ* 53 (1991) 202–20.

Martola, N., *Capture and Liberation: A Study in the Composition of the First Book of Maccabees* (Abo: Abo Akademi, 1984).

Melamed, E. Z., "Josephus and I Maccabees: A Comparison," *ErIsr* 1 (1951) 122–30 (in Hebrew).

Melugin, R., "Muilenburg, Form Criticism, and Theological Exegesis," *Encounter with the Text* (ed. M. J. Buss; Philadelphia: Fortress, 1979) 91–102.

Muilenburg, J., "Form Criticism and Beyond," *JBL* 88 (1969) 1–18.

Nelis, J. T., *1 Makkabeeën* (Roermond: Romen & Zonen, 1972).

Nelson, R. D., "The Anatomy of the Book of Kings," *JSOT* 40 (1988) 39–48.

Neuhaus, G., "Quellen im 1. Makkabäerbuch? Eine Entgegung auf die Analyse von K.-D. Schunk," *JSJ* 5 (1974) 162–75.

———, *Studien zu den poetischen Stücken im 1. Makkabäerbuch* (Würzburg: Echter, 1974).

Oesterley, W., "The First Book of Maccabees," *APOT* 1. 67–123.

Parker, K. I., "The Limits to Solomon's Reign: A Response to Amos Frisch," *JSOT* 51 (1991) 15–21.

———, "Repetition as a Structuring Device in 1 Kings 1–11," *JSOT* 42 (1988) 19–27.

Rajak, T., "Hasmonean Dynasty," *ABD* 3.67–76.

Rhetorical Criticism: Essays in Honor of James Muilenburg (ed. J. J. Jackson and M. Kessler; PTMS 1; Pittsburgh: Pickwick, 1974).

Sachs, A. J. and Wiseman, D. J., "A Babylonian King List of the Hellenistic Period," *Iraq* 16 (1954) 202–11.

Schötz, P. D., *Erstes und Zweites Buch der Makkabäer* (Würzburg: Echter, 1948).

Schunck, K.-D., *1. Makkabäerbuch* (JSHRZ 1/4; Gütersloh: Gerd Mohn, 1980).

———, *Die Quellen des I. und II. Makkabäerbuches* (Halle: Niemeyer, 1954).

Schürer, E., et al., *The History of the Jewish People in the Age of Jesus Christ* (Edinburgh: Clark, 1973–87).

Schwabe, M. and Melamed, E., "Zum Text der Seronepisode in I Macc. und bei Josephus," *MGWJ* 72 (1928) 202–4.

Schwartz, S., "Israel and the Nations Roundabout: 1 Maccabees and the Hasmonean Expansion," *JJS* 42 (1991) 16–38.

Sievers, J., *The Hasmoneans and Their Supporters. From Mattathias to the Death of John Hyrcanus I* (South Florida Studies in the History of Judaism 6; Atlanta: Scholars, 1990).

Sternberg, M., *The Poetics of Biblical Narrative* (Bloomington: Indiana University, 1985).

Tarn, W. W., *The Greeks in Bactria and India* (3d ed.; Chicago: Ares, 1984).

Tcherikover, V., *Hellenistic Civilization and the Jews* (Philadelphia: Jewish Publication Society, 1961).

Tedesche, S. and Zeitlin, S., *The First Book of Maccabees* (New York: Harper & Brothers, 1950).

Trible, P., *Rhetorical Criticism: Context, Method, and the Book of Jonah* (Minneapolis: Fortress, 1994).

Van Selms, A., "The Origin of the Title 'The King's Friend,'" *JNES* 16 (1957) 118–23.

Waard, J. de, "The Chiastic Structure of Amos 5.1–17," *VT* 25 (1977) 170–77.

Walsh, J. T., "Genesis 2:4b–3:24: A Synchronic Approach," *JBL* 96 (1977) 161–77.

———, "Symmetry and the Sin of Solomon," *Shofar* 12 (1993) 11–27.

Walters, S. D., "Jacob Narrative," *ABD* 3. 599–608.

Wellhausen, J., *Israelitische und jüdische Geschichte* (Berlin: de Gruyter, 1921).
Wendland, E. R., "Structural Symmetry and Its Significance in the Book of Ruth," *Issues in Bible Translation* (ed. P. C. Stine; London: United Bible Society, 1988) 30–63.
Wenham, D., "Abomination of Desolation," *ABD* 1. 28–31.
Williams, D. S., "Narrative Art in 1 Maccabees VI 1–17," *VT* 49 (1999) 109–18.
———, "Once Again: The Structure of the Narrative of Solomon's Reign," *JSOT* (forthcoming).
Willrich, H., *Urkundenfälschung in der hellenistisch-jüdischen Literatur* (Göttingen: Vandenhoeck & Ruprecht, 1924).

Index of Ancient Sources

OTHER

Index of Authors Cited

The Catholic Biblical Quarterly Monograph Series (CBQMS)

1. Patrick W. Skehan, *Studies in Israelite Poetry and Wisdom* (CBQMS 1) $9.00 ($7.20 for CBA members) ISBN 0-915170-00-0 (LC 77-153511)
2. Aloysius M. Ambrozic, *The Hidden Kingdom: A Redactional-Critical Study of the References to the Kingdom of God in Mark's Gospel* (CBQMS 2) $9.00 ($7.20 for CBA members) ISBN 0-915170-01-9 (LC 72-89100)
3. Joseph Jensen, O.S.B., *The Use of tôrâ by Isaiah: His Debate with the Wisdom Tradition* (CBQMS 3) $3.00 ($2.40 for CBA members) ISBN 0-915170-02-7 (LC 73-83134)
4. George W. Coats, *From Canaan to Egypt: Structural and Theological Context for the Joseph Story* (CBQMS 4) $4.00 ($3.20 for CBA members) ISBN 0-915170-03-5 (LC 75-11382)
5. O. Lamar Cope, *Matthew: A Scribe Trained for the Kingdom of Heaven* (CBQMS 5) $4.50 ($3.60 for CBA members) ISBN 0-915170-04-3 (LC 75-36778)
6. Madeleine Boucher, *The Mysterious Parable: A Literary Study* (CBQMS 6) $2.50 ($2.00 for CBA members) ISBN 0-915170-05-1 (LC 76-51260)
7. Jay Braverman, Jerome's Commentary on Daniel: A Study of Comparative Jewish and Christian Interpretations of the Hebrew Bible (CBQMS 7) $4.00 ($3.20 for CBA members) ISBN 0-915170-06-X (LC 78-55726)
8. Maurya P. Horgan, *Pesharim: Qumran Interpretations of Biblical Books* (CBQMS 8) $6.00 ($4.80 for CBA members) ISBN 0-915170-07-8 (LC 78-12910)
9. Harold W. Attridge and Robert A. Oden, Jr., *Philo of Byblos,* The Phoenician History (CBQMS 9) $3.50 ($2.80 for CBA members) ISBN 0-915170-08-6 (LC 80-25781)
10. Paul J. Kobelski, *Melchizedek and Melchirešaʿ* (CBQMS 10) $4.50 ($3.60 for CBA members) ISBN 0-915170-09-4 (LC 80-28379)
11. Homer Heater, *A Septuagint Translation Technique in the Book of Job* (CBQMS 11) $4.00 ($3.20 for CBA members) ISBN 0-915170-10-8 (LC 81-10085)
12. Robert Doran, *Temple Propaganda: The Purpose and Character of 2 Maccabees* (CBQMS 12) $4.50 ($3.60 for CBA members) ISBN 0-915170-11-6 (LC 81-10084)
13. James Thompson, *The Beginnings of Christian Philosophy: The Epistle to the Hebrews* (CBQMS 13) $5.50 ($4.50 for CBA members) ISBN 0-915170-12-4 (LC 81-12295)
14. Thomas H. Tobin, S.J., *The Creation of Man: Philo and the History of Interpretation* (CBQMS 14) $6.00 ($4.80 for CBA members) ISBN 0-915170-13-2 (LC 82-19891)
15. Carolyn Osiek, *Rich and Poor in the Shepherd of Hermes* (CBQMS 15) $6.00 ($4.80 for CBA members) ISBN 0-915170–14-0 (LC 83-7385)
16. James C. VanderKam, *Enoch and the Growth of an Apocalyptic Tradition* (CBQMS 16) $6.50 ($5.20 for CBA members) ISBN 0-915170-15-9 (LC 83-10134)

17. Antony F. Campbell, S.J., *Of Prophets and Kings: A Late Ninth-Century Document (1 Samuel 1-2 Kings 10)* (CBQMS 17) $7.50 ($6.00 for CBA members) ISBN 0-915170-16-7 (LC 85-12791)
18. John C. Endres, S.J., *Biblical Interpretation in the Book of Jubilees* (CBQMS 18) $8.50 ($6.80 for CBA members) ISBN 0-915170-17-5 (LC 86-6845)
19. Sharon Pace Jeansonne, *The Old Greek Translation of Daniel 7-12* (CBQMS 19) $5.00 ($4.00 for CBA members) ISBN 0-915170-18-3 (LC 87-15865)
20. Lloyd M. Barré, *The Rhetoric of Political Persuasion: The Narrative Artistry and Political Intentions of 2 Kings 9-11* (CBQMS 20) $5.00 ($4.00 for CBA members) ISBN 0-915170-19-1 (LC 87-15878)
21. John J. Clabeaux, *A Lost Edition of the Letters of Paul: A Reassessment of the Text of the Pauline Corpus Attested by Marcion* (CBQMS 21) $8.50 ($6.80 for CBA members) ISBN 0-915170-20-5 (LC 88-28511)
22. Craig Koester, *The Dwelling of God: The Tabernacle in the Old Testament, Intertestamental Jewish Literature, and the New Testament* (CBQMS 22) $9.00 ($7.20 for CBA members) ISBN 0-915170-21-3 (LC 89-9853)
23. William Michael Soll, *Psalm 119: Matrix, Form, and Setting* (CBQMS 23) $9.00 ($7.20 for CBA members) ISBN 0-915170-22-1 (LC 90-27610)
24. Richard J. Clifford and John J. Collins (eds.), *Creation in the Biblical Traditions* (CBQMS 24) $7.00 ($5.60 for CBA members) ISBN 0-915170-23-X (LC 92-20268)
25. John E. Course, *Speech and Response: A Rhetorical Analysis of the Introductions to the Speeches of the Book of Job, Chaps. 4 - 24* (CBQMS 25) $8.50 ($6.80 for CBA members) ISBN 0-915170-24-8 (LC 94-26566)
26. Richard J. Clifford, *Creation Accounts in the Ancient Near East and in the Bible* (CBQMS 26) $9.00 ($7.20 for CBA members) ISBN 0-915170-25-6 (LC 94-26565)
27. John Paul Heil, *Blood and Water: The Death and Resurrection of Jesus in John 18 – 21* (CBQMS 27) $9.00 ($7.20 for CBA members) ISBN 0-915170-26-4 (LC 95-10479)
28. John Kaltner, *The Use of Arabic in Biblical Hebrew Lexicography* (CBQMS 28) $7.50 ($6.00 for CBA members) ISBN 0-915170-27-2 (LC 95-45182)
29. Michael L. Barré, S.S., *Wisdom, You Are My Sister: Studies in Honor of Roland E. Murphy, O.Carm., on the Occasion of His Eightieth Birthday* (CBQMS 29) $13.00 ($10.40 for CBA members) ISBN 0-915170-28-0 (LC 97-16060)
30. Warren Carter and John Paul Heil, *Matthew's Parables: Audience-Oriented Perspectives* (CBQMS 30) $10.00 ($8.00 for CBA members) ISBN 0-915170-29-9 (LC 97-44677)
31. David S. Williams, *The Structure of 1 Maccabees* (CBQMS 31) $7.00 ($5.60 for CBA members) ISBN 0-915170-30-2

Order from:

The Catholic Biblical Association of America
The Catholic University of America
Washington, D.C. 20064